Declan Greene is a writer and theatre-maker based in Melbourne, Australia. His plays include *A Black Joy* and *Moth*, and have been produced at the Malthouse, Sydney Opera House and Brisbane Powerhouse. Awards include the Max Afford Playwrights Award, the Malcolm Robertson Prize, the R.E. Ross Trust Playwright's Development Awards (2007 and 2009), the AWGIE for Theatre for Young Audiences, the Green Room Award for Best Original Writing (2010), and a nomination for the Helpmann Award for Best New Work. Commissions include Melbourne Theatre Company, Malthouse, HotHouse and Arena Theatre. Alongside Ash Flanders he runs independent theatre company Sisters Grimm, and has co-devised work including *Mommie & the Minister*, *Little Mercy* and *Summertime in the Garden of Eden*, touring locally and overseas. In 2012 his play *Pompeii, L.A.* will debut at the Malthouse Theatre.

Pip Edwards as Dorothy and Josh Futcher as De Silva in the 2009 Little Ones Theatre Production of Home Economics *at the The Store Room, Fitzroy, Melbourne. (Photo Stephen Nicolazzo)*

MOTH
&
Home Economics

DECLAN GREENE

CURRENCY PLAYS

First published in 2012
by Currency Press Pty Ltd,
PO Box 2287, Strawberry Hills, NSW, 2012, Australia
enquiries@currency.com.au
www.currency.com.au

Reprinted 2023

NATIONAL LIBRARY OF AUSTRALIA CIP DATA

Author:	Greene, Declan.
Title:	Moth & home economics / Declan Greene.
ISBN:	9780868199405 (pbk.)
Subject:	Friendship—drama.
	Bullying—drama.
Dewey Number:	A822.4

Publication of this title was assisted by the Commonwealth Government through the Australia Council, its arts funding and advisory body.

Contents

Typeset by Dean Nottle for Currency Press.
Printed by Hyde Park Press, Richmond SA.
Cover image: (front) Jose William Vigers; and (back) Carly Hulls in the 2009 Little Ones Theatre Production of *Home Economics* at the The Store Room, Fitzroy, Melbourne (Photo: Stephen Nicolazzo).
Cover design by Katy Wall for Currency Press.

For Jo & Nyall

Declan Greene's Excruciating Theatre

> There can be a blurry line between laughing at the expense of a character and laughing at the recognition of something painful and true.
>
> *Todd Solondz*

Welcome to the excruciating theatre of Declan Greene. It's painful and it's true. It's vicious and merciless. It is populated by flawed, often unlikeable characters, drowning in dramatic irony. It is brutal and often ugly, and bad things happen to bad people and good people alike. It can be hard to watch but compels you not to look away.

On the flipside, Declan's world is also hilarious, compelling and never nasty for the sake of it. It inhabits the blurry line between cruelty and empathy, eschewing easy targets in favour of catching the bigger fish, exposing the hypocrisies and little tyrannies in which we all indulge. His humour is that of recognition and discomfort. It is dark satire with no easy 'outs', in the lineage of Joseph Heller, Sandra Bernhart and Todd Solondz.

In these two plays, written around the same time but very different in form and intent, we see that his worlds can be excruciating in very different ways. *Moth* is a suburban tragedy in which the audience bears witness to the mental and social unravelling of a troubled boy and the consequences for the friend who has been left behind to process the grief and guilt. *Home Economics* is a suite of grotesque vignettes bound by the related subjects of sexual dependency and food. In both of these plays we see a writer mining the darker, private regions of the human psyche, perhaps seeking to provoke buried thoughts in the minds of the audience, exposing hypocrisies that lay behind social mores and challenging audiences' perceptions of their own moral superiority.

Moth was originally commissioned by Arena Theatre Company and Malthouse Theatre, as a new work for teenage audiences. When I first approached Declan Greene with the idea of a commission, I didn't know a lot about his work. I had read *Rageboy*, a sparkling, kitsch satire touching on organised religion, adolescence and family dysfunction.

I had started to hear a lot about the Sisters Grimm, his high-camp, queer, trash-tribute-band of an independent theatre company making low-rent shows in pop-up venues around Melbourne. I hadn't seen any of their shows. All I knew was little snatches of film uploaded onto their website and YouTube. This was an entirely appropriate way to become acquainted with this group of artists, emerging as they had in the age of sound bites, viral celebrity and democratised Culture. From these grainy clips I gleaned a raw performance style, an unmediated relationship between artists and audience—they seemed more like party dares than shows. They always looked as if they might fall apart completely. At the same time there was never any danger of this, as they had always already fallen apart, in some way. The other thing I got from these shakily shot snippets was dialogue that was very witty—snappy, fierce and merciless in its pursuit of its targets. The cleverness of the dialogue belied the rough, anti-aesthetic surface, buying the trust that is implicit in a solid contract between audience and artist.

The other key element to the Sisters Grimm aesthetic was their abiding fondness for trashy Camp. These guys were sifting through trash not because they liked getting filthy (although that would have been part of it), but because rifling through someone's trash reveals a lot about them. And sifting through the trash of a society, we learn a lot about how that society operates. Witness this in the films of John Waters and Todd Solondz, the performance art of Karen Finley and the photography of Nan Goldin. For Declan Greene and his cohorts, Camp trash culture has provided a fertile ground for a vicious satire, sophisticated art in the gaudy clothing of Camp. In his work with the Sisters Grimm and early commissions for university theatres, this has been the artistic pulse of Declan Greene. A bin-diver, a trash-lover, but above all, a satirist.

Given that this was my introduction to his work, on the surface it's odd that I came to approach him with an idea for writing a contemporary tragedy for teenage audiences. Declan's work showed an abiding love of Camp. Susan Sontag famously argued that Camp is the antithesis of tragedy; that Camp's tonality of excruciating recognition denies the catharsis of tragedy. But I had good reason to approach him. I felt that the tragedy part of creating a new work would be something we could work on together. However, a flair for sparkling, witty dialogue and a mature understanding of theatrical form were things that a writer had to bring to the table themselves. I have found these qualities hard to find together in young writers. At any rate, I wasn't sure it would work out, but a hunch is hunch and there's no harm in having a coffee and a conversation, which is how we started.

So we met for coffee, talked about theatre and I put on the table some thoughts I'd been having about some starting points for a new play. I was interested to see if they sparked any interest with him. I wanted to know if his obvious talents might be harnessed towards tragedy, without sacrificing the wit and vicious satire that had brought him to my attention. I presented a few starting points. Firstly, the location of school cricket nets on the edge of a school oval at night. Secondly, the idea that religious insight and mental illness might in some way be the same thing, seen through different lenses. Thirdly, a simple theatrical form in which the actor and the text were primary.

Further background to the discussion was an alarming report I had recently read, in which it was stated that over a quarter of children aged between 10 and 14 in Australia were worried that the world would come to an end before they grow old. Also casting a shadow over early discussions was the very recent event in Melbourne, in which a skinny, disturbed, 15-year-old boy, armed only with a small kitchen knife, was shot dead by police officers in a suburban skate park. I was interested in the blurred line between religious zeal, millennialism and mental illness. On the other hand, I was interested in the fact that so many young people have a genuine fear of global destruction.

The final element throw into the mix was one of my favourite short stories by the master satirist Saki. *Sredni Vashtar* tells the tale of a disturbed young boy who believes a wild ferret living in his backyard is the animal embodiment of a god, and builds a shrine in its honour. His devotion is ultimately repaid when the wild animal savages (and presumably kills) his cruel guardian cousin. It had been in the back of my mind to work on a show in which a similar relationship between child and animal/god might be explored. We discussed a few manifestations of this, before Declan landed on the figure of a Moth.

Through a series of emails, we decided on some central characters, a form of storytelling and a plot. We did this the usual way I work with writers on a new concept—I would put forward some fairly average ideas, prompting Declan to come up with something far better. He produced a first draft, which became the basis of three development weeks with actors spread out over a few months. Each of these weeks included visits to a nearby high school, where we tested the play for authenticity of language and characters, engagement value of the plotting and generally made sure that we weren't a bunch of old theatre people misrepresenting or offending the intelligence of young people. The responses were overwhelmingly positive, and contributed to the development of the play. In these workshops, I saw firsthand just how well Declan is able to capture the spirit and inner life of teenage characters and the sometimes tyrannical world of the high school campus.

Through the seven weeks of development and rehearsal, with the aid of some extraordinary actors and creatives, Declan created a gripping, honest, terrifying and brutally funny play that has connected deeply with audiences of different ages. From the start, he was adamant that we resist making the central characters of Sebastian and Claryssa likeable. He was also adamant that the play not attempt to falsely provide easy answers to some of the hardest aspects of growing up. I think writers, directors and actors can spend too much time worrying about the likeability of their characters. We don't need to like anyone on stage to be gripped by the world. Integrity of purpose, authenticity of voice and identification will win out every time.

I think that *Moth* is something of an anomaly in Greene's work to date. It occupies its own little space, conspicuously eschewing Camp and excess as driving elements. His work with Sisters Grimm is grounded in a very sophisticated and finely tuned understanding of Camp tradition, whether it is riffing off Blaxploitation movies, Tennessee Williams or Hannie Rayson. This was never discussed, but I think it was a very deliberate choice by Declan to allow the work to grab the audience by the throat and not allow them any release through ironic detachment. In *Moth*, it is almost as if Camp crumbles under the weight and urgency of two teenagers in extreme mental distress.

Sitting in the audience for the very first performance of *Moth* stands out as one of my most treasured experiences in the theatre. We had spent four or five preview performances making numerous cuts and additions, both large and small, attempting to find the right shape for the work. The actors were incredibly committed and generous, incorporating these changes into their performances from day to day. By the time the show opened, I don't think that any of us really knew exactly what it was. But by the end of the first performance, it was clear to me that Declan had succeeded in creating a compelling tragedy, taking the audience on a thrilling and, at times, harrowing ride. Its most shattering moments are the ones where we see the characters unable to see themselves from outside of the positions that they are stuck in: Sebastian, idolising his tormentors and showing disdain for the people who have his best interests at heart; Claryssa, locked in a kind of purgatory where she attempts to make sense of the unthinkable, the survivor grappling with guilt and questions of her own part in the loss of a young life.

Home Economics is a different beast. It offers four snapshots of microcosms populated by thoroughly abject individuals. In this satire, Declan has chosen to present four fragments of narratives, all middles with no beginnings or ends. In doing so, he denies the audience the satisfaction of discovering possible resolutions, disastrous or upbeat. He opts to present characters and the situations that they are in, leaving it to the audience to imagine what might have led to these situations, or in what direction they might head.

The character list reads as a rollcall of people we might be glad we are not—a morbidly obese man and his feeder girlfriend, a home economics teacher struggling with paedophilic cravings, a 'man-hungry' gay 14-year-old, a sugar-addicted girl with rotting teeth and limited self-concept, a deeply misogynistic john, and so on. Their language, actions and relationships may provoke responses of disgust and panic in the audience. But this is no freak show. Rather than holding the characters up for ridicule, Declan approaches then with honesty and authenticity, affording them the complexity necessary for identification and empathy to take hold. The characters are also given space to demonstrate an awareness of their place in relation to accepted norms and power structures, but not the agency to adapt to or challenge these norms. Often this self-awareness is buried deep in the subtext, but it is there nonetheless, and it redeems the characters. By positioning the characters in relation to the power structures that underpin society, the audience is prompted to consider their own position. Who are we to judge? To what laws, universal or otherwise, are we holding these characters to account?

The best satire profoundly understands its targets. It sets out to reveal the tyranny that lies behind a taboo, or a hypocrisy that hides behind an assertion of authority. But to do so effectively, it needs to understand the attraction of this tyranny or this hypocrisy—the writer can never allow themselves to stand outside the value system that allows or demands that these injustices be perpetuated. So the satirist has a bit of disdain for their subject, and a bit of admiration. In Declan's writing, there is always a sense of him loving the thing that he is tearing apart, because without this dialectic, there is emptiness, consumption, pastiche. This is certainly evident in *Home Economics*.

So, congratulations for buying, borrowing, stealing or downloading this book. Read these plays—I hope you like them. By the way, if you don't like one of them, it is still quite possible that you will like the other, as they are quite different to each other. Between them they represent two very different positions in the Declan Greene continuum of Tragedy and Camp. But however one chooses to categorise them, like all of Declan's plays, they are funny and terrible and, when they really hit their stride, excruciating.

I recommend reading these plays out loud, with friends. If you have time and all the correct permissions, please put them on stage in front of an audience, where they really belong. Like Genies in a lamp, they lay in wait, hoping that a director, some actors and an audience will release them from the page and bring them to life again.

Chris Kohn
April 2012

Chris Kohn is Artistic Director at Arena Theatre Company, North Melbourne.

Sarah Ogden as Claryssa in the 2010 Arena Theatre Company production of Moth *at the Malthouse Theatre, Melbourne. (Photo Jeff Busby)*

Sarah Ogden as Claryssa and Dylan Young as Sebastian in the 2010 Arena Theatre Company production of Moth *at the Malthouse Theatre, Melbourne. (Photo Jeff Busby)*

MOTH

Moth was first produced by Arena Theatre and Malthouse Theatre at The CUB Malthouse, Melbourne, on 13 May 2010 with the following cast:

SEBASTIAN	Dylan Young
CLARYSSA	Sarah Ogden

Director, Chris Kohn
Set & Costume Designer, Jonathan Oxlade
Lighting Designer, Rachel Burke
Composer, Jethro Woodward
Dramaturg, Maryanne Lynch
Audio Visual Designer, Domenico Bartolo

THANKS

Nick Pease and the students of Buckley Park Secondary College. Christian Leavesley, Erin Milne, Jaclyn Booton, Michael Kantor, Stephen Armstrong. The actors who developed *Moth* over 2009: Eryn-Jean Norvill, Chris Ryan, Jada Alberts, Ash Flanders, Sarah Borg. Claudio Tocco, for his support and patience over the year this play was written. And my endless gratitude to Chris Kohn, for the opportunity to work with him.

CHARACTERS

SEBASTIAN, 15, terminally unpopular anime devotee. Impossibly skinny and gawky with big bug-eyes. He wears a second-hand school blazer that is several sizes too big, with shorts and a shirt, no tie. His head is shaved and he has a rash of pimples across his forehead. His skin is always slightly greasy. He drowns himself in Lynx deodorant because he gets B.O. and has an organically intense smell. His laugh is beyond annoying. He is obsessed with video games and post-apocalyptic anime—'Ghost in the Shell', 'Neon Genesis Evangelion', 'Akira', 'Trinity Blood', et cetera.

CLARYSSA, 15, deliberately unpopular 'emo' art-freak. She is tall and overweight and wears a massively oversized school jumper to camouflage her weight, with sleeves that hang way down over her hands. Her hair is dyed black with an inch of brown regrowth, and is always frizzy and untamed. Out of school uniform she would wear a toned-down version of Goth regalia—tight black jeans, dog-collar, black lipstick, et cetera. She hates everyone in her year-level—thinks they're all fuckheads, and has no problem with people hating her.

SETTING

The play is set within two separate memories of a specific time frame. Both Sebastian and Claryssa help enact each other's recollections.

NOTES

A forward-slash / indicates where the next line starts to overlap.

When Sebastian or Claryssa play another character—or each other—it is not the actor assuming a different role. Their portrayal is entirely subjective, very much mediated by their opinion of that person at that time. An integral part of the friendship between Sebastian and Claryssa is their love of mocking each other and the people around them, so this should be taken into consideration as well.

Words within quotation marks are a memory of words that were spoken. Words out of quotation marks are in the present.

There are two possible endings to *Moth*. The inclusion of Scene Seventeen in production is optional.

Total darkness.

Then—a huge halogen floodlight begins to flicker.

SEBASTIAN *and* CLARYSSA *appear suddenly, frozen: holding hands, staring up at the light in terror and wonder. The light flickers on them like a strobe.*

The light flickers off.

SCENE ONE

CLARYSSA *and* SEBASTIAN, *side by side.*

SEBASTIAN *stares at* CLARYSSA.

CLARYSSA *looks away, ignoring him.*

SEBASTIAN: Hey.

Pause.

Hey, Claryssa. Hey.

Pause.

CLARYSSA *ignores him.*

CLLLLaryssa. CLLLL—[*searching*]—Chlorine. CLLLL—[*searching*]—Chlamydia. CLLLL—[*searching*]—Clearasil. Ha-ha, Clearasil.

Pause.

[*Softly*] Claryssa. Claryssa.

Pause.

[*Loudly*] CLARYSSA!

Pause.

Are you ignoring me, Claryssa?

Pause.

Claryssa, are you ignoring me?

Pause.

SEBASTIAN *takes a huge breath—his cheeks puff out.*

There is a long pause.

Gradually his face turns red.

CLARYSSA: Stop it, Sebastian.
Stop it.
I'm not talking to you.
I'm not talking to you, no matter what. So you can just give up right now.
You hear me? Stop it.

His face turns purple.

Sebastian. SEBASTIAN!
Stop it, Sebastian!
STOP IT! STOP IT! SEBASTIAN, STOP IT!

He pleads with her.

FINE!

SEBASTIAN *exhales, laughing.*

So annoying.
SEBASTIAN: Ha-ha-ha.
CLARYSSA: So fucking annoying.
SEBASTIAN: Yes, you are.
CLARYSSA: Your head looks disgusting when you do that.
SEBASTIAN: Does it?
CLARYSSA: It looks like you're going to pop.
SEBASTIAN: Sweet.
CLARYSSA: Shut. Up.
SEBASTIAN: Are you angry at me?

Pause.

Are you angry at me, Claryssa?
CLARYSSA: No.
SEBASTIAN: Are you sure you're not angry?
CLARYSSA: Yes.
SEBASTIAN: But are you SURE you're / not angry—?
CLARYSSA: I'M NOT ANGRY, YOU PIECE OF SHIT! I'M SAD! OKAY?! I'M FUCKING SAD!
SEBASTIAN: [*pretending to cry*] Awwww!

CLARYSSA: SHUT. UP.

SEBASTIAN: AWWWW! Cheer up, emo kid! / Cheer up! Cheer up! Cheer up!

CLARYSSA: I swear, Sebastian. I swear. If you don't shut the fuck up right now I'll kick your ass.

SEBASTIAN: You'll what?

CLARYSSA: I'll kick your ass.

SEBASTIAN: You'll… You'll lick my ass?

CLARYSSA: I'll KICK your ass.

SEBASTIAN: You'll lick my ass?

CLARYSSA: I'll KICK your ass!

SEBASTIAN: You'll lick my ass?

CLARYSSA: I'll KICK YOUR ASS!

SEBASTIAN: That's gross. Why would you even want to lick my ass?

CLARYSSA *punches him.*

SCENE TWO

SEBASTIAN: AHHHHHH!

AHHHH, that HURT.

CLARYSSA: Oh my God. You're such a fucking pussy.

SEBASTIAN: Whatever. It's not my fault you've got huge guns.

She punches him again.

AHH! Claryssa! That was exactly the same spot!

CLARYSSA: *PUSSY. / Huge, huge, gigantic—*

SEBASTIAN *coughs violently.*

Pause.

CLARYSSA *holds out a handkerchief.*

Spit.

She holds out a handkerchief. He spits into it.

SEBASTIAN: Is it…?

CLARYSSA: Blood.

SEBASTIAN: A lot?

CLARYSSA: Quite a lot.

SEBASTIAN: I feel okay.

CLARYSSA: You look okay.

SEBASTIAN: Can you not ignore me please? It's rude.

She punches him again.

OW! Can you stop it?!

CLARYSSA: You're so fucking clueless!

SEBASTIAN: What?

CLARYSSA: You think this is fun for me?

SEBASTIAN: What did *I* do?

CLARYSSA: SHUT UP, SEBASTIAN!

Beat.

Whenever they talk about you at school… whenever I hear your name, even… I feel sick. I feel so, so sick. Like my heart spewed up.

SEBASTIAN giggles.

SHUT UP.

Beat.

And the thing is… I think about you… all the time.

I just… I close my eyes… I start to drift… And I'm—

Floodlight.

SEBASTIAN: [*whispered*] 'Claryssa. Claryssa.'

CLARYSSA: I'm in my bedroom. And there's a tapping at the window.

SEBASTIAN: 'Talk to me, Claryssa. Claryssa. Please talk to me.'

Pause.

CLARYSSA: And then we're back here. We're back at the start. And we have to do it all over again.

SEBASTIAN: Do what again?

CLARYSSA: Right from the start.

SEBASTIAN: Do what? What is it?

CLARYSSA: I can't tell you.

SEBASTIAN: Why?

CLARYSSA: Because you won't want to do it.

SEBASTIAN: Why?

CLARYSSA: Because it hurts.

SEBASTIAN: So?

CLARYSSA: And you're a pussy.

SEBASTIAN: You're the pussy. I'm hella bad.

CLARYSSA: You are a pussy. You're a pussy and a loser and a—

SEBASTIAN: Well, at least I'm not a psycho.

CLARYSSA: Well, at least I'm not a retard.

SEBASTIAN: Tool!

CLARYSSA: Loner!

SEBASTIAN: Bitch!

CLARYSSA: Prick!

SEBASTIAN: EMO!

CLARYSSA punches him in the head.

AH!

CLARYSSA: 'CLINTON, YOU FAGGOT!'

SEBASTIAN: What was that for, you crazy bitch?!

CLARYSSA: It wasn't me—it was Clinton.

SEBASTIAN: Oh.

CLARYSSA: Throwing shit at you.

SEBASTIAN: Aww, it's a sandwich!

CLARYSSA: 'FUCKWIT!'

SEBASTIAN: It's tuna! I'm gonna stink!

CLARYSSA: And he's all like—'SORRY SEBASTIAN! I WAS AIMING FOR THE BIN!'

SEBASTIAN: And you're all like—[*shrieking*] 'THAT'S NOT EVEN FUNNY, YOU FAGGOT!'

CLARYSSA: I don't sound like that.

SEBASTIAN: Ha-ha. Yes you do.

She hits him.

AWW!

CLARYSSA: 'STOP THROWING SHIT, YOU BOGAN FUCK.'

SEBASTIAN: [*Clinton*] 'STOP SITTING NEXT TO THE BINS, YOU FUCKIN' EMO.'

CLARYSSA: 'I'M NOT AN EMO, I'M A WICCAN, FUCKHEAD!'

SEBASTIAN: [*Clinton*] 'YOU'RE A FUCKIN' PSYCHO. THAT'S WHAT YOU ARE!'

CLARYSSA: 'WHY DON'T YOU GO FUCK YOURSELF.'

SEBASTIAN: [*Clinton*] 'WHY DON'T YOU GO CUT YOURSELF.'
Ha-ha.

CLARYSSA: Shut up, Sebastian.

SEBASTIAN: What? He's funny!

CLARYSSA: 'I'm actually going to kick his ass. Hold my sausage roll.'

SEBASTIAN: 'Can you not be so embarrassing?!'

CLARYSSA: 'Excuse me?'

SEBASTIAN: 'You're making us look lame.'

CLARYSSA: 'As if I care.'

SEBASTIAN: 'As if you don't.'

CLARYSSA: 'I don't give a shit what those fuckheads think of me. They're just jealous haters.'

SEBASTIAN: 'Ha-ha. Yeah, Clinton's so jealous of you.'

CLARYSSA: 'He is!'

SEBASTIAN: 'He so wishes he was a weird emo with no friends.'

CLARYSSA: 'At least I'm not povo scum.'

SEBASTIAN: 'Shhh!'

CLARYSSA: 'With a dad in jail.'

SEBASTIAN: 'Shut up! He'll hear you!'

CLARYSSA: 'You've just got no balls.'

SEBASTIAN: 'I'm sorry they're not massive like yours.'

She hits him.

CLARYSSA: 'CLINTON! THAT'S A FUCKING ROCK!'

SEBASTIAN: 'NO, THAT'S COOL! I'M COOL, BRO! HA-HA-HA!'

CLARYSSA: 'THAT'S ASSAULT, CLINTON!'

SEBASTIAN: [*Clinton*] 'WHAT YOU GONNA DO? GONNA CALL THE COPS?'

CLARYSSA: 'THAT'S RIGHT, FUCKHEAD! I'M GONNA CALL THE

COPS! AND YOU CAN GO TO JAIL AND GET RAPED LIKE YOUR DAD.'

Beat.

SEBASTIAN: Oh, shit.

Pause.

CLARYSSA: And he comes over. And he stands over us.

SEBASTIAN: He's so tall…

CLARYSSA: 'WHAT ARE YOU GONNA DO, CLINTON? GONNA HIT A GIRL?'

Clinton punches SEBASTIAN *in the mouth.*

SEBASTIAN *collapses.*

'Shit! Are you okay?'

SEBASTIAN *mumbles something, his mouth covered.*

'What did you say?'

SEBASTIAN: [*venomously*] 'You fat fucking psycho.'

Pause.

SCENE THREE

CLARYSSA: The rest of the day is bullshit. In art class… All I can I think about is taking the razor from my art kit… and sticking it right into my arm.

She grins.

Like, cutting it up, blood everywhere. And then going up to you… And unwrapping the bandage… And shoving it in your face. And screaming, like—'See what you made me do, Sebastian?! See what you made me do?!'

Beat.

SEBASTIAN *giggles.*

But Mr Paglos comes over.

SEBASTIAN: Wow, that's lucky.

CLARYSSA: I would have done it.

SEBASTIAN: Sure you would have.

CLARYSSA: He's all like—

SEBASTIAN: 'What are you drawing, Claryssa?'

CLARYSSA: And I'm like—

SEBASTIAN: [*Claryssa*] 'Oh, you know. Just some stupid lesbian.'

CLARYSSA: It's Angelina Jolie.

SEBASTIAN: [*Claryssa*] 'So everyone thinks I'm weird and bisexual even though I'm not.'

CLARYSSA: Get fucked, Sebastian!

SEBASTIAN: [*Mr Paglos*] 'And what's that on her hand?'

CLARYSSA: 'Her third eye.'

SEBASTIAN: 'And what's coming out of the eye?'

CLARYSSA: 'Blood.'

SEBASTIAN: 'Blood. And wasn't the assignment, Claryssa, wasn't the actual assignment to draw someone else in the class?'

CLARYSSA: 'Um, yes. It's called artistic freedom.'

SEBASTIAN: 'That's not what we're studying. We're studying charcoal.'

CLARYSSA: 'Oh, my God, how inspiring.'

SEBASTIAN: 'Well, I think you can just start again, please.'

CLARYSSA: 'This is bullshit!'

SEBASTIAN: 'LANGUAGE, please!'

CLARYSSA: 'No-one in this class deserves to be drawn by me!'

SEBASTIAN: 'Well, maybe you'd like to draw the inside of Ms Muir's office!'

CLARYSSA: 'MAYBE YOU'D LIKE TO DRAW THE INSIDE OF MY ASS.' And he gives me a detention. Just for not confirming to his retarded fucking lesson plan.

SEBASTIAN: Ha-ha.

CLARYSSA: I go home.

SEBASTIAN: And I go home. The house is all dark. The curtains are closed, so that's a bad sign. Mum's in the dark. I can hear her sniffing. I try to sneak past but straight away she hears me and goes—

CLARYSSA: 'Sebby?'

SEBASTIAN: 'Yeah?'

CLARYSSA: 'Come here.'

SEBASTIAN: 'Okay.'

Pause.

CLARYSSA: 'How was your day?'

SEBASTIAN: 'Okay.'

CLARYSSA: 'How was school?'

SEBASTIAN: 'Okay.'

CLARYSSA/MUM *cries more.*

Uhh… 'Is something wrong?'

CLARYSSA: 'No. I'm fine.'

SEBASTIAN: 'Okay.'

Beat.

'Hey I'm gonna go / watch—'

CLARYSSA: 'Lenny broke up with me.'

SEBASTIAN: 'Oh. That sucks.'

CLARYSSA: 'I really, really liked him, Sebby.'

SEBASTIAN: Don't make her cry like that.

CLARYSSA: Like what?

SEBASTIAN: You're making her look lame.

CLARYSSA: 'I don't know what went wrong.'

SEBASTIAN: 'Yeah. I don't know either.'

CLARYSSA: 'We had such a good connection. You know? He really *listened* to me.—And the sex…'

SEBASTIAN: HEY!

CLARYSSA: 'The sex was mind-blowing.'

SEBASTIAN: She didn't say that!

CLARYSSA: Yes she did.

SEBASTIAN: Well, you're making it sound weird.

CLARYSSA: It is weird.

SEBASTIAN: YOU'RE WEIRD.

CLARYSSA: Thank you.

SEBASTIAN: 'Don't worry. You'll find someone else.'

CLARYSSA: 'Will I?'

SEBASTIAN: 'Yes.'

CLARYSSA/MUM *hugs* SEBASTIAN.

Ugh, get off me, Claryssa!

CLARYSSA: 'What's that smell?'

SEBASTIAN: 'Tuna.'

CLARYSSA: 'It's all over you. Look.'

SEBASTIAN: 'Yeah. I fell on it.'

CLARYSSA: 'Oh.'

Beat. Then, she resumes crying…

'What am I going to do, Sebby?'

SEBASTIAN: Go up to my room. Lay on my bed. I'd watch TV—like *Trinity Blood* or something but the TV's next to Mum and that means I'd have to talk to her. So I start tracing instead.

CLARYSSA: Oh, my God.

SEBASTIAN: This sweet-ass panel from *Neon Genesis*. It's the Fourteenth Angel—Zeruel—floating over Tokyo-3 with this huge skull-face, shooting out a tractor beam and exploding whole buildings into itty bitty pieces. All these people screaming, 'THE END IS NIGH'. And when I finish it looks pretty sweet. Like, really sweet, I gotta say.

CLARYSSA: You're such a fuckhead.

SEBASTIAN: What?

CLARYSSA: Um, it's tracing. It's not hard. You're not a genius.

SEBASTIAN: Yeah, well, it looks like what it's supposed to look like.

CLARYSSA: Like that's hard.

SEBASTIAN: Like your drawings actually look like Angelina Jolie.

CLARYSSA: FUCK. YOU.

SEBASTIAN: And then my phone beeps.

CLARYSSA: 'meet me at the oval in twenty'

SEBASTIAN: And I figure, whatever. It's better than being here.

CLARYSSA: Oh, gee, wow, thanks.

SEBASTIAN: You're welcome, Claryssa.

CLARYSSA: Suck my dick.

A flash of light.

SCENE FOUR

Night-time, floodlit.

CLARYSSA: School at night is so fucking creepy. Totally deserted. Like everyone's dead. Like it's the end of the world, and we're the only people left. We walk between the buildings and our footsteps echo. I think how weird it is to see you outside school. Weird, but nice. Really nice.

SEBASTIAN: 'Stop looking at me like that.'

CLARYSSA: 'Like what?'

SEBASTIAN: 'I don't know. Just stop it.'

CLARYSSA: We walk across the oval. Out toward the floodlights. Not even talking. Just pulled here. Pulled out towards the light.
'Surprise.'

SEBASTIAN: 'What?'

CLARYSSA: 'We're going to a party.'

SEBASTIAN: 'Lame. I'm going home.'

CLARYSSA: 'Shut up. It'll be good.'

SEBASTIAN: 'Who's going?'

CLARYSSA: 'I don't know. I saw it on Facebook, it looks good.'

SEBASTIAN: 'Will there be Xbox?'

CLARYSSA: 'No, but there'll be poetry readings, and a séance, and—'

SEBASTIAN: 'Ha-ha-ha!'

CLARYSSA: 'Shut up, fuckwit! Like you know what's cool!'

SEBASTIAN: 'I'm going home.'

CLARYSSA: 'No you're not. Take the bottle.'

SEBASTIAN: 'I don't want it.'

CLARYSSA: 'Just drink it—Jesus! Stop being such a pussy!'

SEBASTIAN: 'I don't want any. It burns!'

CLARYSSA: 'Get a grip, Sebastian—it's just Malibu.'

SEBASTIAN: 'Can't we just drink the Fanta?'

CLARYSSA: 'Oh, my God, you're so embarrassing.'

SEBASTIAN *drinks, retches.*

'Can you do me a favour and not talk to anyone tonight.'

SEBASTIAN: 'Oh, yeah. 'Cause emos are so cool.'

CLARYSSA: 'They're not emos. They're Wiccans, fuckhead.'

SEBASTIAN: ' "Hey, everyone! Let's get high and pretend to be witches!" '

CLARYSSA: 'I AM A WITCH.'

SEBASTIAN: ' "Let's listen to Marilyn Manson and touch each other's boobs!" '

CLARYSSA: 'You know what? Fuck you. You're banned from the coven.'

SEBASTIAN: 'You don't have that power.'

CLARYSSA: 'You're not coming.'

SEBASTIAN: 'I'm coming.'

CLARYSSA: 'No way.'

SEBASTIAN: 'I'm coming.'

CLARYSSA: 'No!'

SEBASTIAN *takes a huge breath and holds it, with his cheeks bulging.*

'That's not going to work.'

He holds it.

'You don't even want to come! You're just doing it to annoy me!'

Pause.

'SEBASTIAN! SEBASTIAN!'

His face starts to go red.

'FINE! Fine! You can come.'

He exhales, giggling.

SEBASTIAN: 'This is going to be so lame.'

CLARYSSA: 'Fuck you're annoying.'

SEBASTIAN: 'Will everyone be dancing around a cauldron?'

Pause.

CLARYSSA: Then you say…

SEBASTIAN: I can't remember.

CLARYSSA: It's all blurred, fuzzy around the edges. Hours pass. We're lying on the grass. Head to head in the floodlight. We're laughing. And it feels good. It feels right.

'Hey… If you could have one wish… what would it be?'

SEBASTIAN: 'I don't know.'

CLARYSSA: 'And don't say something lame. Like, "A force field." '

SEBASTIAN: 'Oh, man—that would be sweet. Yeah, a force field.'

CLARYSSA: 'You're such a fuckhead.'

SEBASTIAN: 'I wish for a force field.'

CLARYSSA: 'You know what I'd wish for?'

SEBASTIAN: 'Lipo?'

CLARYSSA: 'No.'

SEBASTIAN: 'Liposuction?'

CLARYSSA: 'NO. SHUT UP.'

'I'd wish for a bomb. Just a huge atom bomb I could drop on this stupid fucking school and this stupid dumb-ass city.'

SEBASTIAN: 'Ha-ha.'

CLARYSSA: 'And everyone would die. Like, turn to ash. Like—my mum and my dad, and Mr Paglos, and Clinton, and the jocks and the barbie dolls in their little conformist dreamland… Everyone would die. Except for me.'

SEBASTIAN: 'And me.'

CLARYSSA: 'Yeah.'

'Everyone, turned to ash. Except for you and me.'

Then…

SEBASTIAN: I don't know.

CLARYSSA: You feel sick.

SEBASTIAN: 'I feel sick.'

CLARYSSA: 'Stop being a pussy. Drink.'

SEBASTIAN: We laugh…

CLARYSSA *giggles, drunk.*

It gets colder. It's cold.

CLARYSSA: We get closer.

SEBASTIAN: 'Cause I'm cold.

CLARYSSA: Every time we laugh it echoes, right out into the dark.

SEBASTIAN: Then…

CLARYSSA: It's empty.

SEBASTIAN: What?

CLARYSSA: The bottle's empty.

SEBASTIAN: So?

She kisses him.

It is long and messy, teeth bumping together, neither of them certain where to put their hands.

Then, suddenly, the floodlights explode on.

SCENE FIVE

Pause, deeply uncomfortable.

They can't look each other in the eye.

SEBASTIAN: Did you hear them coming?

Pause.

CLARYSSA: They saw it.

Pause.

SEBASTIAN: Way out there. Way out in the dark.
They're cheering. They're clapping.

CLARYSSA: They saw everything.

SEBASTIAN: I want to run.

CLARYSSA: Motherfuckers.

SEBASTIAN: I want to run. Want to hide.

CLARYSSA: Motherfuckers. All of them.

SEBASTIAN: He steps out. Into the floodlight.
His weird bug eyes. All red and wet and…
'Clinton.'
Oh, fuck.
And out in the dark—all of them—Fisher and Turner and Wade… wrestling and falling and screaming on the grass.

CLARYSSA: There's a cold breeze.

SEBASTIAN: [*whispered*] 'Claryssa…'

CLARYSSA: A plane's flying over somewhere.

SEBASTIAN: 'Claryssa…' He grins really huge—

CLARYSSA: [*Clinton, loudly*] 'HELLO SEBASTIAN!'

SEBASTIAN: And then he looks at you.

CLARYSSA: [*Clinton, loudly*] 'HELLO DOGGY!'

'WALKING THE DOG, HEY SEBASTIAN? ARE YOU TAKING THE DOG FOR A WALK?'

SEBASTIAN: 'Ha-ha. Ha-ha.'

'I guess, yeah.'

CLARYSSA: [*Clinton*] 'WE'RE NOT INTERRUPTING, ARE WE?'

SEBASTIAN: 'No! Ha-ha! No. No way.'

CLARYSSA: [*whispered*] Motherfucker.

CLARYSSA: [*Clinton*] 'NO, PLEASE. RETURN TO WHAT YOU WERE DOING BEFORE WE INTERRUPTED YOU.'

SEBASTIAN: 'We weren't doing anything.'

CLARYSSA: [*Clinton*] 'YES YOU WERE. YOU WERE MAULING HER, YOU LITTLE FUCK. YOU WERE MAULING THAT DOG.'

SEBASTIAN: 'Ha-ha. No way!'

CLARYSSA: Motherfucker.

SEBASTIAN: 'She mauled me.'

CLARYSSA: Motherfucker.

SEBASTIAN: 'As if I'd do that.'

CLARYSSA: [*Clinton*] 'YOU DON'T NEED TO BULLSHIT ME, SEBASTIAN. I'M TOTALLY COOL WITH BESTIALITY. I FUCK MY DOG ALL THE TIME.'

SEBASTIAN: I send you a trillion telepathic messages.

CLARYSSA: 'FUCKING YOUR DOG IS REALLY, REALLY RAD, MAN.'

SEBASTIAN: Claryssa. Claryssa. Do something. Do something.

CLARYSSA: Motherfucker. Motherfucker.

'IS THAT WHAT YOU WERE DOING, SEBASTIAN? FUCKING YOUR DOG?'

SEBASTIAN: 'Um. I dunno. Yeah?'

Pause.

Then, he grins. He grins real sick.

Pause.

CLARYSSA: 'IS SHE ON HEAT?'

SEBASTIAN: I wanna spew.

CLARYSSA: [*weakly*] Please.

SEBASTIAN: Wanna spew. Wanna cry.

CLARYSSA: Please. Just don't fucking answer him.

SEBASTIAN: 'I DON'T KNOW. PROBABLY. HA-HA.'

Beat.

CLARYSSA: 'YOU KNOW HOW YOU CAN TELL?'

SEBASTIAN: 'NO.'

CLARYSSA: 'YOU KNOW HOW YOU CAN TELL IF A DOG'S ON HEAT?'

SEBASTIAN: 'NO.'

CLARYSSA: 'IT'S THE WARMTH GIVEN OFF ITS GENITALS. DID YOU KNOW THAT?'

SEBASTIAN: 'HA-HA. NO. I SURE DIDN'T KNOW THAT.'

CLARYSSA: 'THE WARMTH GIVEN OFF BY ITS SLIT, IT'S TRUE.'

Beat.

'MAYBE YOU'D LIKE TO FEEL FOR US, SEBASTIAN.'

SEBASTIAN: 'Ha-ha…'

CLARYSSA: 'WOULD YOU LIKE TO DO THAT FOR ME, MATE?'

SEBASTIAN: 'Ha-ha…'

CLARYSSA: 'I THINK I'D LIKE YOU TO DO IT.'
'DO IT.'

SEBASTIAN: 'NO WAY. GROSS. I DON'T WANT TO TOUCH HER THING.'
You're crying. I look at you—

CLARYSSA: Don't look at me.

SEBASTIAN: You look away.

CLARYSSA: 'DO IT. TOUCH THE DOG.'

SEBASTIAN: Help me. Help me. He grabs my hand.

CLARYSSA: 'TOUCH IT. TOUCH IT.'

SEBASTIAN: And suddenly—you look up at me.
'Claryssa?'
Right into me.

Beat.

You say—

CLARYSSA: [*whispered*] 'Faggot.'

SEBASTIAN: And he says—

CLARYSSA: [*Clinton*] 'WHAT DID SHE SAY?'

Pause.

'I said don't you dare fucking touch me, faggot.'

Beat.

[*Clinton*] 'OWNED! OH, MY GOD—FUCKING OWNED!'

SEBASTIAN: Claryssa?

CLARYSSA: 'THAT'S SO FUCKING RAD!'

SEBASTIAN: Why would you—?

CLARYSSA: 'OWNED!'

SEBASTIAN: Why would you—?

CLARYSSA: 'FUCKING. OWNED.'

SEBASTIAN: Claryssa?

CLARYSSA: 'GET HIS LEGS.'

SEBASTIAN: Someone pushes me—

CLARYSSA: 'I'M NOT TOUCHING HIM.'

SEBASTIAN: Someone laughs.

CLARYSSA: 'HE FUCKING STINKS.'

SEBASTIAN: It's retarded, it's retarded—

CLARYSSA: [*Clinton*] 'I SAID—TAKE HIS LEGS.'

SEBASTIAN: But all I can think is—

CLARYSSA: [*Clinton*] 'HOLD HIS LEGS—'

SEBASTIAN: All I can think is—

CLARYSSA: 'HOLD HIM DOWN.'

SEBASTIAN: I wish I had a force field—

CLARYSSA: [*Clinton*] 'SIT ON HIS ARMS.'

SEBASTIAN: I wish I had a force field—

CLARYSSA: [*Clinton*] 'GET YOUR PHONE—'

SEBASTIAN: I wish I had a force field—

CLARYSSA: [*Clinton*] 'I WANT YOU TO FILM THIS…'

SEBASTIAN: Something lands on my face.

CLARYSSA: Spit.

SEBASTIAN: Another—another.

CLARYSSA: Globs of spit.

SEBASTIAN: You're there but it's not you.

CLARYSSA: I want—I want—

SEBASTIAN: What happened to your face?

CLARYSSA: I want them… to hold your nose.

SEBASTIAN: It's all wrong.

CLARYSSA: To open your mouth.

SEBASTIAN: Falling—I'm—

CLARYSSA: To spit down your throat.

SEBASTIAN: I'm a puddle—I—

CLARYSSA: To see you—

SEBASTIAN: I—ripple—

CLARYSSA: And choke and—

SEBASTIAN: I'm hot and—

CLARYSSA: Choke and—

SEBASTIAN: I'm hot, I'm hot—

CLARYSSA: Choke and choke—

SEBASTIAN: I'm on fire and—

CLARYSSA: I want it so bad it makes me sick.

Beat.

SEBASTIAN: His face is floating over me.

CLARYSSA: I walk away.

SEBASTIAN: 'CLARYSSA?'

CLARYSSA: Into the dark.

SEBASTIAN: 'CLARYSSA?'

CLARYSSA: I walk away and I don't look back.

SEBASTIAN: Then…

Beat.

SCENE SIX

Static.

SEBASTIAN: This explosion, the back of my head…

CLARYSSA: Initiating first-level interface.

SEBASTIAN: I'm falling back, feel myself falling… I'm gonna hit the ground.

Pause.

But I don't.

CLARYSSA: Stabilising pressure.

SEBASTIAN: I don't hit the ground. I just keep falling… Falling through light—this amazing warm light—this—tingling—

CLARYSSA: Bio-port docking.

SEBASTIAN:—at the base of my spine.

CLARYSSA: Flooding neural synapses.

SEBASTIAN: Pouring all through me—

CLARYSSA: All systems go. Prepare for launch.

SEBASTIAN: And this… this is when he appears.

'Sebastian.'

Hanging in the light. A hundred feet tall. Bigger than I can even see. Plated in this, like, mecha-armour… Steam hissing out from the joints. He looks mostly android, I guess—but his chest is open, all meat and blood… Sick. A pair of lungs, filling with fluid. A heart beating in hot blue flame.

I know his name.

'Sebastian.'

Same as my name.

'My sweet child Sebastian.'

And I've never been so scared in my life.

'Don't be scared. I won't harm you.'

'Are you an Angel?'

'I am Saint Sebastian—the nineteenth Angel. Harbinger of a bitter prophesy.'

'Are you my guardian angel?'

'No. I am a destroying angel.'

'Whoa. That's… really, really sweet.'

'I have come to you with a task. A most wonderful and terrible task.'

'What? For me?'

'Yes, Sebastian. For you. Especially for you.'

And the port in the back of my spine tingles.

'Soon I am to descend. And your world is to be destroyed.'
And then I see it. I actually see it all. There's fire raining from the sky. People in the streets, eaten with flames, screaming as they burn. Rats streaming around their feet, rats fleeing—
'What is this?'
'This is Holy Fire, Sebastian. The flame that cleanses.'
'Why are you showing me this?'
'This is your destiny. To save mankind. To usher them into the safe and awaiting arms of the Lord.'
'But how? What do I do?'
'You will know.'
'No, I don't know anything. I'm really dumb.'
And then—it starts to split…
'Do not doubt yourself.'
It flickers like a TV, like a billion globes are burning out—
'No, but I'm dumb. I've really dumb. I've never got better than a C-plus. Please—'

A burst of static.

But his voice is slipping—it's fading away—
'Have faith, Sebastian. This is a desperate world. But even in these darkest of times, there is still hope for mankind.'
'No, but / what do I do?—What do I do—?'
'You are that hope, Sebastian. You alone are pure enough for this solemn task.'
'Wait!—Sebastian? Sebastian?!'

SCENE SEVEN

SEBASTIAN: But everything splits…

An electrical charge: flickering, building in intensity.

Saint Sebastian breaks into a trillion tiny pieces, these pieces of light, flapping against the dark. And they're screaming. And they're all around me. Clouds of dust rise as they swarm…
Moths.
A trillion moths all around me—smacking against my face, in my

nostrils, crawling and crunching against one another… I try to scream—I try to scream but they pour in my mouth—they pour down my throat—filling my chest—and I cannot breathe, I try to gag, the dust, the dust, I cannot breathe I cannot scream I cannot breathe I close my eyes I cannot breathe I cannot breathe I cannot breathe I CANNOT I CANNOT I CANNOT I CANNOT—!

SEBASTIAN *jolts upright.*

He gasps, gulping for air.

Pause.

I'm… in a bed.
My bed.
Totally dark. I can see the numbers on my alarm… 3:23 a.m.
It's all here. These noises… Hum of the computer fan. Car drives past.
TV through the floor… Mum's fallen asleep.
Then—a noise.

CLARYSSA *flicks the jar—plink.*

A noise I don't… I don't recognise…

Plink.

I reach over…

Plink.

Switch on the light.

Plink.

And… there's a jar.

Plink.

A big… glass… jar… with a screw-on lid.

Plink.

On my desk.

Plink.

And inside.

Plink.

A moth.

Throwing itself against the glass. Still for a moment. Still for a moment. Then—

Plink.

Still.
Still.
Then—

Plink.

I put my face right up to the jar. It stares back at me. Red eyes, like two beads of blood.

Pause.

'It's you. Isn't it?'
And I know it is. He's here with me. Watching me. Making sure I do good, I do right.
We sit through the night. His jar on my knee. We watch the sunrise together.
I will do good. I will do right. Believe me. Yes. I will do right.

Soft lights come up—dawn.

SCENE EIGHT

Pause.

SEBASTIAN *stares at* CLARYSSA. *She is ignoring him again.*

SEBASTIAN: Claryssa! Hey, did you see that, Claryssa?

Pause.

Claryssa?

Pause.

Claryssa?

Pause.

Claryssa?

Pause.

He takes a huge breath.

CLARYSSA: Fucking piece of shit.

SEBASTIAN: That's better. HA-HA-HA! That's better, Claryssa!

Pause.

Claryssa? Claryssa?

Pause.

You've got to admit, though. That was pretty sweet.

CLARYSSA: That was retarded.

SEBASTIAN: No it wasn't!

CLARYSSA: That was completely, totally fucking retarded.

SEBASTIAN: Shut up!

CLARYSSA: You're a little boy.

SEBASTIAN: Shut up, Claryssa!

CLARYSSA: Who had a dream about a robot. About saving the world.

SEBASTIAN: As if it was a dream!

CLARYSSA: And I thought you fucking cared about me.

SEBASTIAN: Excuse me, Claryssa, but that was *not* a dream. Didn't you see it?

Pause.

Claryssa?

Pause.

Claryssa?

CLARYSSA: I'm not going any further.

SEBASTIAN: What?

CLARYSSA: I'm not going any further. This is bullshit.

SEBASTIAN: No, but we have to!

CLARYSSA: I don't have to do anything. I can just sit here. See?

SEBASTIAN: No—Claryssa! I have to keep going! I'm saving the world, he told me to! Come on—get up, get up!

He tries to pull her up.

Oh, my God—how much do you weigh?

CLARYSSA: FUCK OFF!

He starts coughing.

Pause.

Spit.

He spits in her handkerchief.

Pause.

SEBASTIAN: We have to keep going, Claryssa.
Claryssa. We have to keep going.

Pause.

SCENE NINE

CLARYSSA: I wake up and I can't get out of bed. I actually can't get out of bed. My doona weighs a thousand tonnes and Mum has to drag it off me.

SEBASTIAN: 'Out of bed now, please.'

CLARYSSA: 'No.'

SEBASTIAN: 'School, madam.'

CLARYSSA: 'I'm not going.'

SEBASTIAN: 'You're going. Why aren't you going?'

CLARYSSA: 'Because.'

SEBASTIAN: 'Because why?'

CLARYSSA: 'Because I'M SAD, okay?'

SEBASTIAN: 'Aww. Cheer up, emo-kid.'

CLARYSSA: [*venomously*] Fuck you, Sebastian.

SEBASTIAN: HA-HA!

CLARYSSA: I want to spew. Even just the thought of seeing your face. Hoping it's bruised. Hoping it's smashed up. Hoping they broke the stupid thing in half.

SEBASTIAN: I wake up and it's amazing. And I look outside and it's amazing. And I go to school and for the first time ever I don't feel sick when I walk in the gates. I want to stand on top of the principal's car and yell, 'I AM BETTER THAN ALL YOU FUCKHEADS.' But I don't do that. I don't do that, for now.
I head to our place by the bins. All around me, kids drinking Red Bull, listening to iPods, talking to each other. Like nothing's wrong. Like the world's not ending. Like there isn't a saint in a jar right in front of them.

Then I see you. [*Waving*] 'Hey.'

CLARYSSA: And I see you. [*To herself*] 'Fuck.'

SEBASTIAN: And I can't wait to tell you.

Pause.

SEBASTIAN *sits down.*

CLARYSSA: I wait for it.

Pause.

I WAIT for it.

Pause.

'I'm sorry, Claryssa.' Say it.

Pause.

'I'M SORRY, CLARYSSA.' FUCKING SAY IT, SEBASTIAN, FUCKING—

Pause.

SEBASTIAN: 'So. I bet you can't guess what happened to me last night.'

Pause.

'Do you give up?'

Pause.

'Do you give up?'

CLARYSSA: 'I don't care.'

SEBASTIAN: 'Okay, you give up. Last night—'

CLARYSSA: 'I DON'T FUCKING CARE, SEBASTIAN!'

SEBASTIAN: 'Jesus, what crawled up your anus?'

Pause.

CLARYSSA: 'I don't want you to talk to me anymore.'

SEBASTIAN: 'Good. As if I even want to talk to you.'

Pause.

Long pause.

'Wait… For real?'

Pause.

'Hey no but… Claryssa, something amazing happened last night. I saw—I saw an angel. A real live angel. He was a robot. Kind of. And he said all this stuff—all this stuff about, like, fire and—and I have to do something but I don't really know what I—'

CLARYSSA: 'Can you please go away.'

SEBASTIAN: 'Go where?'

CLARYSSA: 'I don't know. Anywhere. Just not near me.'

Pause.

SEBASTIAN *moves two seats down the bench.*

Long pause.

He takes out his lunch and starts to chew it.

SCENE TEN

SEBASTIAN: First period, R.E., and the classroom's so hot I worry about Sebastian suffocating in his jar. I'm stabbing more airholes in the top but I don't know what they eat, I think, 'I wonder what they eat', I think—

CLARYSSA: 'Sebastian?'

SEBASTIAN: Miss. Sweeney.

She hates me. She actually hates me.

CLARYSSA: 'Sebastian. What's that?'

SEBASTIAN: She's only 22. If we travelled through like a space-time wormhole she'd be one of the hot girls in the back row, like Melissa and Bianca. Flicking water at me from their Mount Franklin bottles, going, 'Take a bath, Sebastian. Take a bath, Sebastian.'

CLARYSSA: 'SEBASTIAN.'

SEBASTIAN: 'Huh?'

CLARYSSA: 'Answer me when I talk to you, please.'

SEBASTIAN: 'Okay.'

CLARYSSA: 'What is that thing?'

SEBASTIAN: 'A moth.'

CLARYSSA: 'I can see that. What is it doing in my class?'

SEBASTIAN: Everyone's looking at me.

He giggles.

[*With attitude*] 'You tell me.'

CLARYSSA: 'Okay, I don't have time for your crap today. Put it in your locker, please.'

SEBASTIAN: I go, 'Why don't you put it in YOUR locker?'

And everyone laughs.

CLARYSSA: No they don't.

SEBASTIAN: 'Fuck you.'

CLARYSSA: 'WHAT DID YOU JUST SAY?'

SEBASTIAN: Whoa, did I just say that or think that?

CLARYSSA: 'OUT. NOW. WAIT OUTSIDE.'

SEBASTIAN: I walk out through the class, everyone laughing.

And I laugh too 'cause soon they'll be dead. Ha-ha.

Outside it's way hot. A couple of Year Sevens walk past in their blazers ten sizes too big. They stop talking when they get near me. They look down, scared. Ha-ha.

'Hey.'

CLARYSSA: 'Hey.'

SEBASTIAN: Ha-ha. Their voices are really high.

'Hey—come here a sec.'

CLARYSSA: 'Why?'

SEBASTIAN: 'I wanna talk to you.'

CLARYSSA: 'You're talking to me now.'

Beat.

SEBASTIAN: Aren't Year Sevens supposed to be scared of Year Nines?

'You're gonna die soon.'

CLARYSSA: 'What?'

SEBASTIAN: 'You're gonna die soon.'

CLARYSSA: 'What did he say?'

SEBASTIAN: 'Just saying, the world's gonna end, and you're both gonna die.'

Pause.

CLARYSSA: [*screaming*] 'YOU THINK I'M SCARED OF YOU MOTHERFUCKER?!'

SEBASTIAN: 'What?'

CLARYSSA: [*screaming*] 'YOU THINK I'M SCARED OF YOU? I'LL FUCK YOU UP!'

SEBASTIAN: 'Whoa—hey. I was just saying—'

CLARYSSA: 'FAGGOT!'

She spits.

SEBASTIAN: Kids are so angry these days.

CLARYSSA: 'It's too hot for this, Sebastian.'

SEBASTIAN: 'What?'

CLARYSSA: 'You can't have that thing in my class.'

SEBASTIAN: 'What thing?'—Where did *she* come from?

CLARYSSA: 'SEBASTIAN.'

'Are you going to put it away?'

Pause.

SEBASTIAN: 'No.'

CLARYSSA: 'Then you're going to Ms Muir's office. Diary, please.'

SEBASTIAN: I don't think I've ever been this close to her before. [*He giggles.*] She wears so much make-up.

CLARYSSA: She wears *so* much make-up.

SEBASTIAN: [*giggling*] I know! I know! So much!

CLARYSSA: Like, two inches at least.

SEBASTIAN: [*giggling*] YES!

CLARYSSA: Maybe three inches. Maybe—

SEBASTIAN *giggles more, hysterical.*

Maybe her head, under all that… Maybe her head is the size of a golf ball.

SEBASTIAN: [*giggling*] It's just make-up! It's all just make-up! Her head is just—

CLARYSSA: 'You think this is funny?'

SEBASTIAN: 'No.'

Pause. SEBASTIAN *tries to stifle laughter.*

CLARYSSA: 'Are you alright?'

SEBASTIAN: [*giggling*] 'Yes.'

CLARYSSA: 'Is something wrong?'

SEBASTIAN: 'No.'

CLARYSSA: 'Do you want to see the counsellor?'

SEBASTIAN: 'No.'

Pause.

CLARYSSA: 'You want to go home? I could call your mum.'

SEBASTIAN: 'Hey. Do you think I could talk to the class?'

CLARYSSA: 'What?'

SEBASTIAN: 'Is it okay if I say something in front of them?'

CLARYSSA: 'Why?'

SEBASTIAN: 'I want to tell them about, like… God.'

CLARYSSA: 'That's my job.'

SEBASTIAN: 'Yeah, but they don't listen to you.'

Beat.

CLARYSSA: 'Okay. You can go now, Sebastian.'

SEBASTIAN: I walk to Ms Muir's office. And I walk past Ms Muir's office. And I walk to the library. Then, I get a fat, black texta and write in my neatest handwriting—

'THE END IS NIGH.'

I photocopy it two hundred times.

He wanders off, dropping bits of coloured paper everywhere.

CLARYSSA: The rest of the day I don't see you.

SEBASTIAN: 'THE END IS NIGH. THE END IS NIGH.'

CLARYSSA: Lunchtime you're not at the bench. Last period you're not in P.E. Mrs Salloti goes, 'Where's your boyfriend?' and I swear if she wasn't a teacher I'd scratch her fucking face off.

Then in the change room Marita Fazzino goes—

SEBASTIAN: 'Hey, so, I heard Sebastian dumped you.'

CLARYSSA: And she's not a teacher. So I do scratch her fucking face off.

SEBASTIAN: What?

CLARYSSA: 'YOU FAT FUGLY FUCKING—'

CLARYSSA *grabs* SEBASTIAN *by the hair.*

SEBASTIAN: 'AHHHH!'

Beat. She releases him.

Fucking psycho.

Pause.

SCENE ELEVEN

CLARYSSA: When Mum's done yelling at me the first thing I do is log in to Facebook and change my status. '… IS SUSPENDED AND LOVING IT.'

I'm about to logout when a note pops up

SEBASTIAN: 'stop being a psycho. i need to talk to you'

CLARYSSA: I click—DELETE.

SEBASTIAN: Oh, my God—did you just de-friend me?

CLARYSSA: Your name drops off my contact list.

SEBASTIAN: Bitch.

CLARYSSA: It lands in my stomach with a sick little thud.

SEBASTIAN: Psycho. Bitch.

CLARYSSA: Straight away I regret it.

I wonder if you're thinking about me. Plotting ways to win me back.

SEBASTIAN: I'm watching *Neon Genesis*. I'm talking to Saint Sebastian.

CLARYSSA: Great.

SEBASTIAN: On TV, it's Shinji Ikari. And he's sweating. He charges through the city in Eva-01, bashing down skyscrapers, leaping over bridges. He jumps and flies into the evil Angel Leliel, firing a zillion laser shots.

CLARYSSA: Lame.

SEBASTIAN: SHUT UP!

… But Leliel disappears. Eva-01 crashes into darkness. Shinji opens his eyes, sideways on the ground… and through the window of the office building, he sees a girl. She's tied to a stake. Her head is shaved. There's cuts all over it, bits of blood and hair. And flames, too. Lots of flames. People cheer as she burns and burns. Her tongue turns black but she cries out, she says… 'Jesus. Jesus. Must I die here?' Jesus hears her, hanging from his cross. He opens one red eye. There's blood running down his feet, running down the wood. The moment it touches the ground the Angels will rise. The moment, the moment it touches the ground—

CLARYSSA: A note pops up.

Beat.

SEBASTIAN: What?

CLARYSSA: On Facebook. See?

SEBASTIAN: But I'm not… I'm not on Facebook, I'm watching a—

CLARYSSA: Yes you are.

SEBASTIAN. Interests: Anime, *The Butterfly Effect*, Hanging out. No new wall posts. Nineteen friends.

'Sebastian has been tagged in a video.'

SEBASTIAN: Really?

Beat.

I click it.

CLARYSSA: It opens.

SEBASTIAN: And it's Clinton's page—Huh?

CLARYSSA: There's a title, three words. 'FAG GETS PWNED.'

I press PLAY.

SEBASTIAN: And it's all pixelated and shitty. You can hardly see anything 'cause the phone's shaking so bad. There's all these guys laughing in a pile. Then the phone tilts up and—

CLARYSSA: The floodlights.

Pause.

SEBASTIAN: And it's me.

CLARYSSA: On the ground. In close-up. Your face slicked with spit. Your eyes rolling around in your skull. Clinton hocks up a glob and it lands on your bottom lip. He's laughing. And you're laughing. But your eyes…

SEBASTIAN: Ha-ha…

CLARYSSA: Thirty-three people 'like' this video.

SEBASTIAN: Fifteen people have commented on this video.

CLARYSSA: 'who's the faggot crying'

SEBASTIAN: 'his name is sebastian he's in year 9'

CLARYSSA: 'i had to sit next to him once in assembly he's got really bad B.O.'

SEBASTIAN: 'he talks to himself in ceramics it's fucking weird'

CLARYSSA: 'he always smells like he's shit himself it's seriously sick seriously'

SEBASTIAN: 'is that the dickhead who hangs out with the emo'

CLARYSSA: 'yep next to the bins LOL'

SEBASTIAN: 'omg why'

CLARYSSA: 'so she can eat from the bin when no-one's looking'

SEBASTIAN: 'NOM NOM NOM LOL'

CLARYSSA: 'no i mean why would anyone hang out with that fugly bitch'

SEBASTIAN: 'LOL WIN'

CLARYSSA: 'i've been wanting to get that faggot for years'

SEBASTIAN: 'omg clinton you shouldn't have done that, don't you know that kid is basically retarded?'

Pause.

And then at the bottom, one from you.

CLARYSSA: I write: 'excuse me but i am not friends with that little fuckwit he hangs off me it's seriously embarrassing'.

Pause.

SEBASTIAN: I logout.

CLARYSSA: I close the browser window. And it's me staring back. The wallpaper on my desktop. I'm like… seven or something. I'm smiling, hugging my sister, and she's smiling too.

And just for a second… I see myself from above. I see myself, right now. This fat… mean… gross… fucking… emo. Who beats up girls. Who has no friends. With a half-eaten block of Crunch sitting on the desk next to her.

I blow out my incense. I throw my candles in the bin. Then I sneak into Mum and Dad's ensuite, and I take a sleeping tablet.

I crawl way down, way deep down—metres below the earth. It's hot with my breath and the earth's core. A cave with the softest walls—my zodiac-print doona. I curl up around my pillow, and wait to go to sleep.

Pause.

SEBASTIAN: He stares at me from his jar. His eyes are as red as the eyes of my alarm clock. Three twenty-three. Four twenty-three. I try to trace but I can't hold the pen steady. I try to read but I can't focus my eyes. I try to relax but my brain relaxes and thoughts spill out in every direction.

A mess of voices.

I keep the lid on the jar. I keep the moth plinking inside but it's getting harder, it's, it's getting harder, it's—
'Saint Sebastian?'

Pause.

'This will probably come as a surprise to you, but… I'm not actually very popular. Most people don't really listen to me.'
'I don't know if I can do this.'
'I don't know if you picked the right person.'
'Saint Sebastian? Saint Sebastian?'

Pause.

Claryssa?

CLARYSSA: Mmm…

SEBASTIAN: Wake up, Claryssa.

CLARYSSA: No.

SEBASTIAN: Why are you being such a bitch to me?

Pause.

The sun comes up. Mum's making breakfast downstairs. I can't go to school or they'll take him from me. I can't stay home or she'll know I'm wagging.

SCENE TWELVE

SEBASTIAN: I put on my uniform. 'Bye, Mum, I'm off to school as usual.' I get the bus but I don't get off. I sit and watch the road whip by, stop after stop, and I wait for it to take me to people who will listen. I'm spacing out when the engine turns off and the driver yells—

Beat.

Claryssa, wake up! The driver yells—

CLARYSSA: [*groggy*] 'Last stop.'

SEBASTIAN: Today I will hand out the flyers. Yes. I will hand out the flyers. And I will use all my power and all my charm to make the world listen.

'The end is nigh. The end is nigh. Soon he's going to kill you.'

Main street, the war memorial, the skatepark, the cemetery. It's so hot. It's so, so hot, my brain's boiling inside my skull. When I can't walk anymore I sit on the curb. And when I look around I'm totally, totally lost. I tap the jar—'Where am I?' But he doesn't know or he doesn't say. Every sign is in some weird language. Except one. Across the road.

CLARYSSA: 'JESUS WILL GUIDE YOU.'

SEBASTIAN: And under that.

CLARYSSA: 'AIR-CONDITIONED.'

SEBASTIAN: I cross the road and I step inside and straight away this old guy screams—

CLARYSSA: 'Close the door!'

SEBASTIAN: I do, and I lick my lips really, really, slowly and I try to figure out what the fuck this place is.

It's a room. Just this huge room, lino on the floor. In one corner there's a ping-pong table, all these really old people sitting around it, playing cards. Next to them, this huge obese guy, playing piano kind of shitty. Am I supposed to be here?

CLARYSSA: I don't know.

SEBASTIAN: I wasn't asking you.

CLARYSSA: Whatever.

SEBASTIAN: Then a voice—

CLARYSSA: 'You.'

SEBASTIAN: And this old guy turns to me.

CLARYSSA: 'You. Come here.'

SEBASTIAN: And his eye is all fucked-up. Sick.

CLARYSSA: 'Didn't your mother tell you it's rude to stare.'

SEBASTIAN: 'What?'

CLARYSSA: 'Close your mouth and sit down.'

SEBASTIAN: And I do because he's watching the TV. There's a little girl hugging a dolphin. This cute little girl. One of his eyes is watching it. But sick one is just staring at me. Stop it.

CLARYSSA: [*old guy*] 'Would you like to ask me a question?'

SEBASTIAN: But I don't. I really don't.

CLARYSSA: [*old guy*] 'Why don't you?'

SEBASTIAN: Because his eye is really fucked up. It's fake. It's a fake eye.

CLARYSSA: [*old guy*] 'But it's made of real glass.'

SEBASTIAN: What happened to it? What's wrong with him?

CLARYSSA: [*old guy*] 'Ask me.'

Pause.

SEBASTIAN: 'What happened to your eye?'

CLARYSSA: 'I lost it.'

SEBASTIAN: 'How did you lose it?'

CLARYSSA: 'Saving the lives of many great men.'

SEBASTIAN: 'Were you in a war or something?'

CLARYSSA: 'Yes. I was in a war or something.'
'Would you like to know the last thing I ever saw?'

SEBASTIAN: 'Okay.'

CLARYSSA: 'A line of ants. Marching across the concrete. Carrying little crumbs of bread on their backs.'

Pause.

SEBASTIAN: 'Then what happened?'

CLARYSSA: 'A gunshot.'

SEBASTIAN: 'Oh.'

CLARYSSA: 'Then—darkness, for a long, long time. Until you came through that door.'
'What are you doing here?'

Pause.

SEBASTIAN: 'I don't know.'

CLARYSSA: 'Come on. You came here for something.'

SEBASTIAN: 'Air conditioning.'

CLARYSSA: 'No. No. You came here for something else.'
'Let me guess.'

Pause.

'You had a holy vision. And the world is ending. And no-one will listen to you.'

SEBASTIAN: 'Maybe.'

He laughs and so does the girl and it looks so, so horrible.

'What should I do?'

CLARYSSA: 'Don't ask me. I'm not the one with the answers.'

SEBASTIAN: And he points.

On the wall there's a Jesus. But his heart is all red… A light bulb, glowing. I go, 'That's a picture.'

CLARYSSA: [*screaming*] 'WASH YOUR MOUTH OUT!'

SEBASTIAN: 'What?'

CLARYSSA: 'THAT IS JESUS CHRIST!'

SEBASTIAN: 'Okay.'

CLARYSSA: 'HE LOVES YOU!'

SEBASTIAN: 'Okay.'

CLARYSSA: 'Don't say "okay". He loves you. He died for you. Did you know that? He died for you!'

SEBASTIAN: 'Uh… I guess… '

He's standing up. All of a sudden it's hot in here.

CLARYSSA: 'This is the problem with you teenagers. This is the problem with you *youth*. No sense of sacrifice. You have everything. You have the whole world and still you're not happy.'

SEBASTIAN: 'Uh… I'm… I'm sorry?'

He's so close I can smell his breath and it's sweet, it's sweet, like he's full of chocolate.

CLARYSSA: 'Sacrifice. Sacrifice. Do you know what that means? Do you even know what that means, shithead?!'

SEBASTIAN: It's so hot. It's so hot. My brain is melting.

CLARYSSA: 'Do you want to see? Do you want to see sacrifice? Do you want to see the true meaning of sacrifice?'

SEBASTIAN: Wasn't there air conditioning? Wasn't there a fan? He puts his fingers in his eye socket. Oh, shit.

CLARYSSA: 'This. This.'

SEBASTIAN: And he pulls out his eye.

CLARYSSA: 'THIS is the meaning of sacrifice.'

SEBASTIAN: And the little girl is crying.

CLARYSSA: 'LOOK. LOOK.'

SEBASTIAN: And there's a hole. In his skull. A big red hole.

CLARYSSA: 'LOOK. DON'T YOU DARE LOOK AWAY.'

SEBASTIAN: A tunnel. Stretching back inside his head, way, way back into darkness.

CLARYSSA: 'LOOK.'

SEBASTIAN: And then—in the dark—in the dark of his skull—a bulb starts to glow. A red light. Jesus—his heart, it starts to glow. His chest unfurls, opens up like a flower. And around his ribs, ropes of TNT, wired and fizzing. A fuse soaked in kerosene. His mouth soaked in vinegar. His chest glowing, the bulb glowing—flickering—and—and buzzing and—the fuse is burning—the bulb is—burning—the moth and the bulb and the fuse and the—all of them—flickering and flapping and burning and burning and—

It explodes! HA-HA! A BANG! Louder than anything ever! And my soul climbs to Heaven—

CLARYSSA: 'Sebastian?'

SEBASTIAN: It climbs to Heaven on a swarm of moths—

SEBASTIAN *begins to convulse.*

CLARYSSA: 'SEBASTIAN?! SEBASTIAN?!'

SCENE THIRTEEN

Pause.

CLARYSSA: Sebastian?

Pause.

Then, he opens his eyes.

SEBASTIAN: Bitch.

CLARYSSA: [*softly*] Stop it.

Pause.

Are you okay?

SEBASTIAN: Yeah.

I mean… Yeah. I'm better than okay. I'm amazing. It makes sense.

CLARYSSA: No it doesn't.

SEBASTIAN: But it does. It all makes sense, see? I count backwards from seven.

Pause.

[*To himself*] Four, three, two, one… I open my eyes… And it's there, in front of me. The path, right to the end. Jesus Christ, he's waiting for me there. Saint Sebastian too. Sacrifice. The greatest sacrifice. Can you keep a secret, Claryssa?

[*Whispered*] I'm going to make a bomb.

CLARYSSA: I know.

SEBASTIAN: What?! Who told you?

CLARYSSA: Just a guess.

SEBASTIAN: An atom bomb. So bright you can't see anything else. And then it's just you and me, at the end. Everyone else turned to ash.

How do I tell you?

CLARYSSA: You can't.

SEBASTIAN: Why not?

CLARYSSA: I'm in my cave. I'm underground.

SEBASTIAN: But what if I call you?

CLARYSSA: My phone doesn't work down there.

SEBASTIAN: What if I send you a telepathic message?

CLARYSSA: My brain doesn't work down there. It sleeps with the rest of me, all wrapped in cotton wool.

Five metres below the surface it's too dark to see myself. Which is perfect, really—the perfect place to be. Under the stars, my zodiac doona. I float through space, trailing little pills, the moon smiles down to talk to me…

SEBASTIAN: 'Claryssa. Claryssa.'

CLARYSSA: And his voice sounds just like my dad's.

SEBASTIAN: 'Are you down there, my dear?'

CLARYSSA: 'What do you want?'

SEBASTIAN: 'Claryssa. Your mother and I have had a very long discussion. And we've decided 15 is far too young to be living in a cave. Now, I think it would be best if you came out of there.'

CLARYSSA: 'Sorry, Mr Moon, but no way. I'm staying right here until I'm twenty-one.'

SEBASTIAN: 'But that would be a terrible waste, my dear. Don't you know these are the best years of your life?'

CLARYSSA: 'That's bullshit.'

SEBASTIAN: 'They speed by so fast and then they're gone.'

CLARYSSA: 'That's total bullshit. These years aren't fast, they're slow. They're so fucking slow. Last night, Mr Moon, I had this dream… I was a deep-sea diver. In one of those old-fashioned metal diving suits. I could hardly move, it was so heavy. But I fell, somehow. I fell on my back—and the suit pinned me down. Down onto the sea floor. And I couldn't get up. I couldn't get up. So I just… lay there. Two thousand tonnes of black water above me, the surface so far I couldn't even see the light. And when I woke up, it's funny but… the feeling was exactly the same. And that's the thing. I don't know when it'll end. I don't know when I'll get up again.'

'Can you tell me?'

SEBASTIAN: 'Oh, Claryssa.'

Pause.

'My dear… listen to me. I know the universe can be a cruel and terrible place. And lonely too… terribly lonely. But if being with him makes it more bearable—my dear, you should talk to him.'

CLARYSSA: 'Talk to who?'

SEBASTIAN: 'Come now. I'm the moon. I wasn't born yesterday.'

CLARYSSA: 'He doesn't care about me.'

SEBASTIAN: 'He does, you know. In fact, he needs you. He needs you very much.'

CLARYSSA: 'That's not the same.'

SEBASTIAN: 'It's not romantic, I know. But it's still a kind of love, my dear.'

CLARYSSA: 'Whatever.'

SEBASTIAN: 'To need someone so badly you can't live without them.'

CLARYSSA: 'I can live without him.'

SEBASTIAN: 'Claryssa, my dear. You're in a cave.'

CLARYSSA: 'He can live without me.'

SEBASTIAN: 'For now, perhaps. But not much longer.'

CLARYSSA: 'What?'

SEBASTIAN: 'If you want my advice—you should answer the phone.'

Pause.

CLARYSSA: 'Maybe.'

SEBASTIAN: 'And eat something, my dear. You're wasting away down there, don't you know.'

Pause.

CLARYSSA: I roll over.

That's when I see I've got 27 missed calls from you.

Pause.

I turn off my phone.

Beep.

'It's Claryssa. Leave your destiny after the tone.'

SEBASTIAN: 'Claryssa. I know you're mad but there's going to be an atomic bomb and I thought you and me could be the last ones left. Call me back please because there's not much time and your soul isn't saved yet. There's not much time.'

CLARYSSA: There's something poking into me through all the layers of cotton.

SEBASTIAN: There's not much time.

CLARYSSA: The floodlights. The oval. Your face wet with spit. And next day—that fucking weird moth in a jar. The pain gets sharper, so I crawl deeper into the cave and curl up around my pillow.

But I have… this fucking… terrible dream.

SCENE FOURTEEN

CLARYSSA: It's you. But you're really fucked-up looking. Your lip is cut. Still hasn't healed. You're barefoot, sweat stains down to your ankles. You haven't slept in days. Walking with that moth in a jar, walking the streets. Your backpack ticking.

SEBASTIAN: A metal pipe.

CLARYSSA: Solidax powder.

SEBASTIAN: Magnesium powder.

CLARYSSA: A washer and some duct tape.

SEBASTIAN: Burning hair. The rats are fleeing—

CLARYSSA: This doesn't make sense.

SEBASTIAN: What doesn't make sense?

CLARYSSA: This—what is this? Is it your dream or my dream?

SEBASTIAN: This isn't a dream. It's the future. See? Saint Sebastian is showing me—descending from the clouds…

CLARYSSA: I don't want to be here. I don't want to see you.

SEBASTIAN: His ribs open, his heart in flames, swallowing the city into his chest—I need more time! The man at the hardware store won't sell me a fuse!

CLARYSSA: This is horrible. How do I wake up?

SEBASTIAN: You can't, Claryssa. Ha-ha. You can't. That's the thing. I've been trying for days. I've been—

CLARYSSA: 'Mate?'

SEBASTIAN: Shit.

CLARYSSA: What?

SEBASTIAN: The cops.

CLARYSSA: The cops? What?

SEBASTIAN: Driving up alongside me. They go—

CLARYSSA: 'What's your name, mate?'

SEBASTIAN: [*whispered*] What's my name?
'CLINTON.' Keep walking.

CLARYSSA: 'Clinton?'

SEBASTIAN: 'CLINTON.'

CLARYSSA: 'Clinton what?'

SEBASTIAN: 'CLINTON CLINTONSON.'

CLARYSSA: 'I think your name's Sebastian.'

SEBASTIAN: 'No it's not.'

CLARYSSA: 'I think there's some people looking for you.'

SEBASTIAN: Keep walking. Don't look at them.

CLARYSSA: 'Your mum's worried, mate. Hop in the car.'

SEBASTIAN: Don't look. Don't look. There's a laneway coming up.

CLARYSSA: 'Come on, Sebastian.'

SEBASTIAN: 'I'm Clinton.' Just a metre away. Wait. Wait.

CLARYSSA: 'Hop in the car, mate. We'll take you home.'

SEBASTIAN: And NOW! I run!

CLARYSSA: What?

SEBASTIAN: Down the laneway.

CLARYSSA: What are you doing? Where are you going?

SEBASTIAN: Faster. Faster. They can't catch me.

CLARYSSA: Wake up, come on. Why am I seeing this?

SEBASTIAN: Help me, Claryssa!

CLARYSSA: Shut up, Sebastian! You're not real!

SEBASTIAN: Please Claryssa! I'm sorry! I'm sorry!

CLARYSSA: Fuck—shit—wake up, wake up—

SEBASTIAN: What do I do? What do I do?

CLARYSSA: I don't know!

SEBASTIAN: Hurry, Claryssa!

CLARYSSA: Look! A door!

SEBASTIAN: It's locked.
Open up! Open the fucking door!

CLARYSSA: They're coming, quick!

SEBASTIAN: Oh shit, oh shit, oh shit!

CLARYSSA: They're coming, Sebastian!

SEBASTIAN: The glass gives way.

CLARYSSA: The energy field ripples—

SEBASTIAN: He's grabbing at my shirt—

CLARYSSA: Reach under. Pull the latch—

SEBASTIAN: 'FUCK OFF! GET YOUR HANDS OFF ME! YOU'RE COVERED IN—YOU'RE COVERED IN—'

CLARYSSA: Where are you?

SEBASTIAN: It's bright here, the lights hurt, they sting. It's noisy—can someone turn the volume down?

CLARYSSA: That woman's a nurse.

SEBASTIAN: She's dressed like one.

CLARYSSA: I can't hear what she's saying.

SEBASTIAN: [*yelling*] 'I NEED TO… I HAVE TO… YOU WANT ME TO…'

CLARYSSA: What's that noise?—The ringing—'PAGING DOCTOR…'

SEBASTIAN: [*yelling*] 'YOU WANT ME TO… WHAT?!'

CLARYSSA: Leave. She wants you to leave.

SEBASTIAN: I'm trying to help her.

CLARYSSA: 'GET OUT! GET OUT!'

SEBASTIAN: Don't you know the people here are sick?

CLARYSSA: It's a hospital, Sebastian.

SEBASTIAN: It's disease, it's full of fucking—

CLARYSSA: They're here *because* they're sick.

SEBASTIAN: 'This is no coincidence, you bitch!'

CLARYSSA: No, it's not! Exactly! That's what I said!

SEBASTIAN: 'YOU'RE NOT LISTENING TO ME.'

CLARYSSA: She's pushing you—

SEBASTIAN: It's ending. It's all fucking ending.

CLARYSSA: Pull open the curtain—

SEBASTIAN: 'WHAT ARE YOU HIDING?'

CLARYSSA: A metal tray clatters over—

SEBASTIAN: A woman in a wheelchair vomits up milk—

CLARYSSA: 'SECURITY.'

SEBASTIAN: Baby screaming—'CAN SOMEONE CONTROL HIM?'

CLARYSSA: 'PAGING SECURITY.'

SEBASTIAN: Pull back the curtain, tear it down—

CLARYSSA: 'YOU LITTLE FAGGOT!'

SEBASTIAN: Walk past the showers with your head down, your head down—

CLARYSSA: The smell of—

SEBASTIAN: Hospital—No. [*He sniffs.*] Boys' change room.

CLARYSSA: Where are we? What the hell is that stink?

SEBASTIAN: Lynx Instinct. Sweet, huh?

CLARYSSA: I can't breathe.

SEBASTIAN: Too much man for you?

CLARYSSA: And you're there—

SEBASTIAN: What?

CLARYSSA: On the ground. 'LITTLE CUNT.'

SEBASTIAN: Oh, shit…

CLARYSSA: They're holding you down.

SEBASTIAN: I don't want to be here.

CLARYSSA: 'HE FUCKIN' STINKS. HE NEEDS A BATH.'

SEBASTIAN: Claryssa… Claryssa…

CLARYSSA: They drag you to the urinal. They push you down.

SEBASTIAN: How do we leave?

CLARYSSA: They hold your head against the metal, they flush it over and over and over. 'Take a bath, Sebastian, take a bath, Sebastian…'

SEBASTIAN: I don't want to watch this. I don't want you to see this.

CLARYSSA: There's a vent—

SEBASTIAN: What?

CLARYSSA: In the wall. Can you see it? Pull off the grate. Crawl up, way up—

SEBASTIAN: Into the tube, the plastic tube—

CLARYSSA: What?

SEBASTIAN: It's a slide—a plastic slide—on my hands and knees—slipping with sweat… Climb way up into a little plastic box.

CLARYSSA: It smells like chips in here—smushed-up burger, sick. Where are you?

SEBASTIAN: McDonald's.

CLARYSSA: The playground?

SEBASTIAN: I think so.

CLARYSSA: Are you safe here?

SEBASTIAN: I don't know.

Pause.

I lay on my side. Listen to my heart. There's blood beating up against my eardrums. I try to gather my thoughts together but they spill away from my fingers, they run away like scared mice… Uhh… Metal pipe. Solidax powder. Help me. Help me.

A crack of thunder.

CLARYSSA: Do you hear that?

Pause.

The noise of raindrops hitting the plastic roof.

SEBASTIAN: What does this mean?

CLARYSSA: 'It's the end.'

SEBASTIAN *raises the jar.*

SEBASTIAN: 'What?'

CLARYSSA: 'I am coming, Sebastian.'

SEBASTIAN: 'Saint Sebastian?'

CLARYSSA: 'I am descending.'

SEBASTIAN: 'No! I need more time!'

CLARYSSA: 'You must act quickly.'

SEBASTIAN: I could do it.
I could detonate it here.

CLARYSSA: Don't!

SEBASTIAN: It doesn't matter.

CLARYSSA: They're children!

SEBASTIAN: They'll all die soon enough.

CLARYSSA: 'Excuse me.'

Pause.

SEBASTIAN: Shit.

Pause.

CLARYSSA: 'Is someone down there?'

SEBASTIAN: I was followed. I was fucking followed.

CLARYSSA: 'Sebastian—is that you?'

SEBASTIAN: Who the fuck is it? What do they want?

CLARYSSA: Calm down, Sebastian.

SEBASTIAN: 'WHO THE FUCK IS THERE!'

CLARYSSA: Don't yell—

SEBASTIAN: 'SHOW YOUR FUCKING SELF!'

CLARYSSA: The lights flick on—

SEBASTIAN: It's… my lounge room. Between the wall and the—the TV cabinet. What?

CLARYSSA: Your mum—holding a cricket bat.
She's crying.

SEBASTIAN: She looks retarded when she cries.

CLARYSSA: 'We need to go back, Sebastian.'

SEBASTIAN: Screwed up. Dripping snot. Shut up. Shut up.

CLARYSSA: 'You need to go back to the hospital.'

SEBASTIAN: 'Get out of the way, Mum. I don't have time.'

CLARYSSA: 'We need to get in the car, now. Come on—'

SEBASTIAN: And she's grabbing me—'Don't touch me. I don't have time.'

CLARYSSA: 'You're sick—you need help—'

SEBASTIAN: 'GET OUT OF MY WAY! I HAVE TO DO THIS!'

CLARYSSA: 'Give me the backpack—please—give me the backpack. Don't hurt yourself. Don't hurt anyone. Don't—'

SEBASTIAN: 'GET YOUR FUCKING HANDS OFF ME!'

CLARYSSA: Something smashes—what smashes? What is it?

SEBASTIAN: A vase? A table? I don't know—it's all atoms.

CLARYSSA: What?

SEBASTIAN: It's all just atoms splitting in the end.

CLARYSSA: 'What atoms? Baby, what are you talking about?'

SEBASTIAN: 'YOU ARE TRYING TO DESTROY MY MISSION.'

CLARYSSA: 'I'm calling the police! I'm calling the police!'

SEBASTIAN: Something's changing. In her face.

CLARYSSA: She's cracking. Her skin is peeling away.

SEBASTIAN: Eyes rolling back to the whites—

CLARYSSA: What is she? What is she?

SEBASTIAN: Veins bulging, her skin crawling—

CLARYSSA: I want to wake up, I want to wake up!

SEBASTIAN: Ants are streaming from the hole in her face—

CLARYSSA: Oh my God—she's a monster.

SEBASTIAN: 'You're a monster.'

CLARYSSA: She's here to stop you.

SEBASTIAN: 'You're here to stop me.'

CLARYSSA: 'PLEASE! DON'T DO THIS!'

SEBASTIAN *wields the jar at her.*

SEBASTIAN: 'By the power of Saint Sebastian I cast you back to Hell!'

CLARYSSA: 'Baby! Stop it! Put it down!'

SEBASTIAN: 'We cast you out! We cast you out!'

CLARYSSA: 'Put it down, baby! Please, put it down!'

SEBASTIAN: 'We cast you out!'

CLARYSSA: 'Please, baby—can't you see it's hurting you?'

SEBASTIAN: 'We cast you out!'

CLARYSSA: 'Baby—baby—please—give it to me! PLEASE!'

> CLARYSSA *and* SEBASTIAN *wrestle with the jar. They lose their grip. It falls on the ground—smashes.*
>
> *The moth flies away.*
>
> SEBASTIAN *lunges at her, going to attack. She screams.*
>
> *Then...*
>
> *They both disappear in an incredible white light.*

SCENE FIFTEEN

CLARYSSA: Are you okay?

SEBASTIAN: Yes, thank you.

CLARYSSA: Are you sure?

SEBASTIAN: Yes, I'm sure, thank you.

CLARYSSA: Sebastian. Look at me.

> SEBASTIAN *looks at her.*

SEBASTIAN: Is Mum okay?

CLARYSSA: She's okay.

SEBASTIAN: Did I hurt her?

CLARYSSA: No. She's just scared. She's called the police.

SEBASTIAN: He's gone, Claryssa. He's gone. I'm alone here on Earth and the Earth is burning. 'Saint Sebastian?' 'Saint Sebastian?' Heaven is a trillion light years away and that's a lot of dark matter, a lot of sin between us. How do you get to Heaven?

CLARYSSA: I don't know, Sebastian.
You live a life that's good.

SEBASTIAN: Do you think I've been good?

CLARYSSA: I think you did your best.

SEBASTIAN: The best I've ever got is a C-plus. Is that good enough?

CLARYSSA: I don't think I'm the right person to ask.

> SEBASTIAN *coughs.*

Spit.

He spits into her handkerchief.

SEBASTIAN: Better or worse?

CLARYSSA: Not better.

SEBASTIAN: Okay.

CLARYSSA: We're nearly at the end.

SEBASTIAN: Are we?

CLARYSSA: The next bit is gonna hurt.

SEBASTIAN: Is it?

CLARYSSA: Will you be okay?

SEBASTIAN: I don't know.

Pause.

Can you come with me?

CLARYSSA: I can't.

SEBASTIAN: Why not?

CLARYSSA: Because it's not true.

SEBASTIAN: Please, Claryssa.

Pause.

He gets up.

The jar breaks. Sebastian dies. Mum's crying and my foot is cut. I drag blood out through the night, all over the concrete. And then… I'm at your house. I'm at your window.

A noise of tapping on glass.

[*Whispered*] 'Claryssa. Claryssa.'

'Talk to me, Claryssa. Claryssa. Please talk to me.'

Pause.

SEBASTIAN *waits for her.*

CLARYSSA: And… I answer.

SEBASTIAN: Do you?

CLARYSSA: The echo carries your voice down, all the way down to the bottom.

SEBASTIAN: And what do you say?

CLARYSSA: I say… I say…

'Is that you, Sebastian—bastian—bastian?'

SEBASTIAN: And what do I say?

CLARYSSA: You say…

'It's me.'

SEBASTIAN: And what do you say?

CLARYSSA: I say…

'I've missed you.'

SEBASTIAN: And what do I say?

CLARYSSA: You say…

'I've missed you too.'

SEBASTIAN: Do you say anything else?

CLARYSSA: I say…

'Can you throw me a rope? I think it's time for me to get out of here.'

SEBASTIAN: But I don't have any rope.

CLARYSSA: Yes, you do. You came exactly prepared. You thought of everything. A rope and a pickaxe and a light you wear on your head. And a canary in a cage.

SEBASTIAN: Really?

CLARYSSA: Just in case of gas leaks. You drop down kilometres into the earth.

SEBASTIAN: It must have been scary.

CLARYSSA: It must have been. But when you appear in the cave you don't seem scared at all. You wrap your arms around me. You buckle me into the harness. You tug the rope to make sure it's secure. And we rise up through the dark like angels. Together. Up towards the light.

SCENE SIXTEEN

The floodlight.

SEBASTIAN: Where are we?

CLARYSSA: Back at the oval. Back at the end.

SEBASTIAN: But why are there sirens? Who are these people?

CLARYSSA: It's the police. Remember? The backpack. The bomb.

SEBASTIAN: There's so many of them.

CLARYSSA: They're scared. Their hands are shaking.

SEBASTIAN: They can see my power. They know my passion.

CLARYSSA: I'm scared too, Sebastian.

SEBASTIAN: Take my hand.

CLARYSSA: They're talking to you. They're so far away.

SEBASTIAN: 'Put down the backpack.'

CLARYSSA: 'Don't hurt yourself.'

SEBASTIAN: 'You need to calm down, mate.'

CLARYSSA: 'Mate, you need to calm down.'

SEBASTIAN: 'Follow the sound of my voice.'

CLARYSSA: 'I want to lead you away from this place.'

SEBASTIAN: 'A land of riches awaiting.'

CLARYSSA: 'The night is closing over.'

SEBASTIAN: 'A boiling of the blood.'

CLARYSSA: 'The rats are streaming through the streets.'

SEBASTIAN: 'Cut the skin to save the limb.'

CLARYSSA: 'Let the blood to stop the fever.'

SEBASTIAN: 'Don't you know that kid is retarded?'

CLARYSSA: 'Burn the bodies in a pit.'

SEBASTIAN: 'Hold his legs.'

CLARYSSA: 'Hold him down.'

SEBASTIAN: 'Get your phone. I want you to film this.'

CLARYSSA: 'This is a desperate world, my child.'

SEBASTIAN: 'Touch it. Touch that fuckin' dog.'

CLARYSSA: 'This. This is the meaning of sacrifice.'

SEBASTIAN: 'You are that hope, Sebastian.'

CLARYSSA: 'You alone are pure enough for this solemn task.'

SEBASTIAN: 'Mate, mate, you need to calm down.'

CLARYSSA: 'Mate, you need to calm down, mate.'
They're getting closer.

SEBASTIAN: 'He's not listening. Look at his pupils.'

CLARYSSA: They're inching closer, step by step.

SEBASTIAN: 'I'm warning you, mate.'

CLARYSSA: 'I'm warning you, mate.'

SEBASTIAN: 'Don't make me do this.'

CLARYSSA: 'Don't make me do this.'

SEBASTIAN: 'Final warning.'

CLARYSSA: 'Final warning.'

SEBASTIAN: 'Put down the backpack.'

CLARYSSA: 'Put down the backpack.'

SEBASTIAN: 'GET BACK! GET BACK!'

CLARYSSA: 'Please, mate. We don't want to hurt you.'

SEBASTIAN: 'LISTEN TO ME!'

CLARYSSA: 'We don't want to hurt you.'

SEBASTIAN: 'NO, LISTEN TO ME!'

Pause.

'The world is ending. The world is burning. It's all your fault—all of you. And he picked me. Above everyone, above everyone in the world. To warn you. To save you. But you wouldn't listen. Well, you'll listen now.'

Claryssa, are you ready?'

CLARYSSA: 'Don't do this, mate.'

SEBASTIAN: 'Claryssa?'

CLARYSSA: 'Please don't do this.'

SEBASTIAN: 'Should I do it?'

CLARYSSA: 'I'm giving you until the count of three.'

SEBASTIAN: 'Claryssa? Talk to me, Claryssa!'

CLARYSSA: 'One.'

SEBASTIAN: 'Claryssa?'

CLARYSSA: 'Two.'

SEBASTIAN: 'Claryssa?'

CLARYSSA: I'm not here, Sebastian.

Pause.

SEBASTIAN: Why?

CLARYSSA: Because it's not the truth.

You didn't rescue me. I don't rescue you.

Pause.

SEBASTIAN: What happens now?

CLARYSSA: They say 'Three'.

SEBASTIAN: And then?

CLARYSSA: They shoot you.

SEBASTIAN: Why?

CLARYSSA: Because they think you have a bomb.

SEBASTIAN: I do have a bomb.

SEBASTIAN *opens his backpack. Comics fall out.*

Oh.

Pause.

CLARYSSA: I'm sorry, Sebastian.

SEBASTIAN: Why?

CLARYSSA: Because it's my fault.

SEBASTIAN: It's not your fault, Claryssa.

Pause.

CLARYSSA: Say that again.

SEBASTIAN: [*same intonation*] It's not your fault, Claryssa.

CLARYSSA: Again.

SEBASTIAN: [*same intonation*] It's not your fault, Claryssa.

Pause.

CLARYSSA: Stand over there.

He does.

Pick your nose.

He does.

Eat it.

He does.

Tell me you forgive me.

SEBASTIAN: I forgive you.

Pause.

Long pause.

CLARYSSA: 'Three.'

The floodlights explode on CLARYSSA *and* SEBASTIAN, *impossibly bright for an instant, then darkness.*

SCENE SEVENTEEN

The play could end at this point. Or the following optional scene could be included in production.

SEBASTIAN *is laying on the ground.*

CLARYSSA: Sebastian.

Pause.

Get up, Sebastian.

Pause.

Sebastian. Get up.

Pause.

SEBASTIAN!

Pause.

CLARYSSA *takes a huge breath.*

SEBASTIAN: Don't you dare.

CLARYSSA: Fuckwit.

SEBASTIAN *laughs and then coughs.*

SEBASTIAN: [*his mouth full*] Do you have a hanky?

CLARYSSA *holds out a hanky.*

He spits into it.

Was that…? It tasted like…

CLARYSSA: Blood.

SEBASTIAN: Oh, no way. Gross.

CLARYSSA: Don't be a pussy. It's just a little blood. See?

SEBASTIAN: Sick! Don't make me look at that.

CLARYSSA: Are you okay?

SEBASTIAN: Yeah. I'm fine.

CLARYSSA: You don't look fine.

SEBASTIAN: I'm fine.

Pause.

Stop looking at me like that, you freak.

CLARYSSA: You look… different.

SEBASTIAN: No I don't. Shut up.

Pause.

CLARYSSA: It's weird. Sometimes… I see a photo and I go, is that what he really looked like?

SEBASTIAN: Um—this is what I look like. See?

CLARYSSA: But you looked younger. I think your eyes were further apart… And your hair was different. Did you always part it on that side?

SEBASTIAN: I don't know. Whatever. It's just hair.

CLARYSSA: It's not just hair. It's important.

Pause.

It's like… I'm think I'm remembering. But actually I'm just remembering remembering. And then I'll be remembering remembering remembering… And the colours fade. And the sound gets muffled. And life keeps going… And going… And going…
And maybe one day I won't miss you anymore.
And maybe one day I'll be happy.

Beat.

SEBASTIAN: Or maybe… you'll just be a sad, fat emo forever.

CLARYSSA: Maybe.

SEBASTIAN: Oh, my God, that was a joke. Can you not be so lame?

CLARYSSA: Shut up.

SEBASTIAN: If you miss me so much, why don't you marry me?

CLARYSSA: Be quiet.

SEBASTIAN: You be quiet.

CLARYSSA: Shhh.

SEBASTIAN: You shhh.

Pause.

Claryssa?

Pause.

Oh, my God—did you fart?

Pause.

That's not even funny, Claryssa. That stinks.

Pause.

Claryssa. Claryssa.

Pause.

Are you ignoring me, Claryssa?

Pause.

Claryssa, are you ignoring me?

He takes a huge breath.

The light flickers on the two of them, then shorts out.

THE END

Christopher Roberts as Phillip and Josh Futcher as Mr Lleyland in the 2009 Little Ones Theatre Production of Home Economics *at the The Store Room, Fitzroy, Melbourne. (Photo Stephen Nicolazzo)*

Home Economics

ACKNOWLEDGEMENTS

Thanks to Sarah Giles, who provided the initial spark of inspiration and guided the play through to first draft.

Home Economics was workshopped in 2012, directed again by Stephen Nicolazzo. Our thanks to the cast of this development: Zoe Boesen, Tom Dent, Anna McCarthy, Marcus McKenzie, Sarah Ogden, and Nikki Shiels.

And my biggest thanks to Stephen. An amazing artist, amazing friend, and amazing drinking partner.

Home Economics was first produced by Little Ones Theatre at the Store Room, Melbourne, on 29 September 2009, as part of the Melbourne Fringe Festival, with the following cast:

MR LLEYLAND / TROY / TELEMARKETER / DE SILVA	Josh Futcher
PHILLIP	Christopher Roberts
GERALD / PRISCILLA / RODERICK	Russ Pirie
CAMERON / ALICE / WOMAN ONE	Cat Commander
WOMAN TWO	Carly Hulls
DOROTHY	Pip Edwards

Director, Stephen Nicolazzo
Set Designer, Daiana Voinescu
Costume Designer, Chloe Greaves
Lighting Designer, Katie Sfetkidis
Sound Designer, Keith McDougall

The version of the play published here has been revised from the script produced in 2009.

CHARACTERS

MARTY, 30s, morbidly obese man

BIANCA, 30s, his girlfriend

MR LLEYLAND, 30s, home economics teacher and cub

PHILLIP, 14, man-hungry gay kid

GERALD, 40s, Mr Lleyland's nurturing hus-bear

PRISCILLA, 14, a motor-mouthed sugar-addicted schoolgirl

TROY, 16, sad teen dream

CAMERON, 16, mean teen dream

DE SILVA, 30s, businessman

DOROTHY, 40s, prostitute

NOTES

A forward-slash / indicates where the next line starts to overlap.

If cast gender-blind, *Home Economics* can be performed with a cast as small as three.

1. MEAT

A nice apartment, somewhere in the city. White walls, cream carpet. There are framed prints on the wall. Maybe one of them is that photo of construction workers eating lunch on the beam of a skyscraper.

In the corner of the room is a stained king-sized mattress. And on it, an enormously, morbidly fat man. He is naked except for a huge bedsheet. There are no clothes in the world that would fit him.

This is MARTY.

He clicks around on a brand new laptop computer. His breathing is heavy and laborious.

There is a long pause. Then, he yells offstage...

MARTY: How long now?!

BIANCA: [*offstage*] Three minutes.

MARTY: How many seconds?!

BIANCA: [*offstage*] Twenty… two.

MARTY *continues clicking around.*

There is another long pause. Then, BIANCA *enters.*

She is a squat woman, slightly overweight, wearing office clothes with flat shoes. She has quite a lot of pimples for someone in her thirties. Most of them have a little red scab on the tip.

BIANCA *sits down next to* MARTY, *and turns on the TV.*

MARTY: How long now?

BIANCA: Two minutes.

MARTY: How / many—?

BIANCA: And thirty seconds.

Pause.

BIANCA *watches TV.* MARTY *clicks around on the laptop.*

I hate Catriona Rowntree.

Pause.

She's so frikkin' ugly. She's way too ugly to be on TV. Don't you think?

Pause.

I think she'd be a bitch in real life as well. You can tell by her face. It's the kind of face a bitch has. Don't you think?
Marty?

MARTY: Yeah?

BIANCA: Ugh. Whatevs.

Pause.

Hey, have you taken your insulin?
Marty?

MARTY: What?

BIANCA: Did Saffron do your insulin?

MARTY: No. Can I have an Endone?

BIANCA: Why do you want an Endone?

MARTY: My foot hurts.

BIANCA: No it doesn't.

MARTY: It does.

BIANCA: You know your foot doesn't hurt. You / know it—

MARTY: Yeah, I know. Except it does. It hurts heaps.

BIANCA: Well, you can't take an Endone on an empty stomach. You'll get all weird again.
After dinner. After you've eaten.

MARTY: How long now?

BIANCA: [*laughing*] I don't know! I don't have frikkin' X-ray eyes!

MARTY: I'm starving.

BIANCA: Are you?

MARTY: Starving. Yeah.

BIANCA: I'll do your insulin. Then it'll be ready.

She prepares the syringe.

MARTY *returns to the computer screen.*

'And how was your day, Bianca?'

MARTY: And how was your day, Bianca.

BIANCA: Okay. Boring. You know that guy Kong? The other temp?

MARTY: No.

BIANCA: Yes you do. He was doing the claims forms as the same time as me. And it was really annoying because the job was so boring, but then he hardly ever talked, so it made the job even more boring. You remember?

MARTY: No.

BIANCA: He was a real loser. A really huge loser. You remember?

MARTY: No.

BIANCA: Well, anyway, he killed himself.

MARTY: Did he?

BIANCA: Yep. Over the weekend.

MARTY: Oh.
How'd he do it?

BIANCA: Don't know. They didn't say.
I bet he cut his wrists, though.

MARTY: Why?

BIANCA: I don't know. He just seemed like the kind of person who would cut his wrists if he wanted to kill himself—hold still.

Just before she injects MARTY, *a timer goes off in the next room.*

MARTY: It's ready! Bianca!

BIANCA: Hold still.

MARTY: It's ready!

BIANCA: Yes, I know. I'm not deaf, Marty, FYI.

MARTY: Ugh.

BIANCA: Hold still.

She jabs MARTY *with the syringe. He doesn't react at all.*

All done.

MARTY: It's ready, Bianca.

BIANCA: Give me a kiss.

MARTY: What?

BIANCA: I said, 'Give me a kiss', loser. Then I'll get your dinner.

MARTY: Why?

BIANCA: Because I'm nice and I'm pretty and you want to kiss me.

MARTY: I'm starving.

BIANCA: So? There is such a thing as manners, Marty.

MARTY: But I haven't eaten since / the afternoon.

BIANCA: Fine.

MARTY: And my foot. It / really—

BIANCA: Fine. Forget it. Forget I said anything.

BIANCA *goes to leave. Then...*

MARTY: Wait.

MARTY *extends his lips.* BIANCA *gives him a little peck.*

BIANCA: Back in a sec. You stay there.

BIANCA *leaves the room.*

Pause. MARTY *stares after her with great anticipation.*

After a few moments BIANCA *re-enters. She carries a huge dinner plate, stacked high with a mush made up of mashed potato, peas and mince.*

MARTY: Wow. What is it?

BIANCA: Shepherd's pie.

MARTY: Wow.

BIANCA: There might be some cold bits in it. I didn't want to stir it too much 'cause then it just turns into mush.

MARTY: It's great. It's brilliant. Thank you. Thank you.

BIANCA: You're welcome.

BIANCA *bends down near him and extends her lips.* MARTY *gives her a peck, and then she balances the plate on his stomach.*

He starts eating. She watches.

MARTY: Aren't you eating?

BIANCA: No.

MARTY: How come?

BIANCA: What do you mean 'how come?' I told you how come.

MARTY: No you didn't.

BIANCA: Yes I did, Marty. Yes I did.

MARTY: Are you on a diet?

Beat.

BIANCA: Excuse me?!

MARTY: What? No, just 'cause I thought—!

BIANCA: Like you can talk!

MARTY: No, 'cause you were on that diet last week. / But I—

BIANCA: Last month! That was last month! And I lost two whole kilos, thank-you-for-noticing.

MARTY: Sorry.

Pause. MARTY *eats.*

BIANCA: I told you I wasn't having dinner tonight.

MARTY: Did you?

BIANCA: In my email. Which I sent you. At one o'clock this afternoon.

MARTY: Oh. Yeah. Okay.

BIANCA: 'Oh. Yeah. Okay.'

MARTY: You had—

BIANCA: He remembers *now*.

MARTY: You had lunch in the cafe downstairs. So you don't need dinner, because the portions are so huge.

BIANCA: That's right. Not that you care.

MARTY: I do care.

BIANCA: You didn't write back.

MARTY: I couldn't. The internet was down.

BIANCA: Pffft. Whatevs.

Pause. MARTY *eats.*

Who cares. Who cares if you replied or not. It was still an awesome lunch.

MARTY: Was it?

BIANCA: Yes.

Pause.

It was a 'welcome' lunch. For Christian. The new temp.

MARTY: Who's Christian?

BIANCA: Oh, I must have forgotten to mention him to you. He took Kong's place.

MARTY: Oh, okay.

BIANCA: Oh, okay.

Pause.

He's really nice. Really interesting.

He dresses really different to everyone else in the office. It's so interesting.

Like, he still he wears suit pants and a shirt and tie, like all the other men. But his are older. Vintage. And he slicks his hair back with a comb. And he has a little clip on his tie…

MARTY: He sounds rich.

BIANCA: No, they're not expensive clothes. They're second-hand. He just chooses them, really good, really fashionable.

Pause.

I'm looking forward to seeing what he wears tomorrow.

BIANCA *takes his plate and goes back to the kitchen.*

MARTY: Is he nice?

BIANCA: [*offstage*] He's very nice. Well… he's nice to me.

MARTY: Is he?

BIANCA: [*offstage*] Really nice. Really friendly.

MARTY: Do the other people in the office like him?

BIANCA: [*offstage*] Jhoti likes him. Gay-Daniel likes him.

MARTY: Does Gay-Daniel think he's gay?

BIANCA: [*offstage*] Yes, Gay-Daniel thinks he's gay. But I don't think so. And you know me, I've got a pretty good gay-dar.

BIANCA *re-enters with another plate, piled high with shepherd's pie.*

Why? Do you think he's gay?

MARTY: I don't know him.

BIANCA: Still.

Pause.

I bet you wish Christian was gay, don't you?

MARTY: Why?

BIANCA: Because then he wouldn't be a threat to you.

MARTY: Oh. Right.

Pause.

BIANCA: I know you hate that me and Christian have chemistry. But you don't have to worry. I'm not going to do anything about it. I'm not like that.

MARTY: Okay.

Pause.

BIANCA: Still. You should probably start replying to my emails.

Pause, as BIANCA *balances the plate on his stomach.*

MARTY: I'm sorry, Bianca. I'm sorry I didn't reply.

BIANCA: It's fine.

MARTY: I just couldn't.

BIANCA: Yes you could. Why couldn't you?

MARTY: The internet was down.

BIANCA: Whatever.

MARTY: It's true.

BIANCA: Whatever, Marty. Talk to the hand, 'cause the face ain't listenin'. Why aren't you eating your pie?

MARTY *stares at it.*

MARTY: I'm full.

BIANCA: Great. So, you don't reply to my emails, and then you tell me my cooking's crap.

MARTY: No… I'm just not that hungry.

BIANCA: Yes you are.

MARTY: I'm not. I'm just right. / Except my—

BIANCA: Which is what you say now. But in an hour you'll be complaining you're hungry again.

MARTY: I won't. It's just my foot.

BIANCA: Your foot doesn't hurt, Marty.

MARTY: But I've got food in my tummy now. Can I take an / Endone?

BIANCA: You can have an Endone when you finish your dinner.

MARTY: I've finished / my—

BIANCA: I don't want you getting funny, Marty. Five more spoonfuls.

Pause.

MARTY *takes a spoonful.*

And FYI, Marty, I know the internet wasn't down. Because I checked the weather on the *Age* website before I left for work.

MARTY: It wasn't working when I woke up.

BIANCA: You don't have to lie.

MARTY: It's true.

BIANCA: Then how come you were on eBay when I came home, then? Huh?

MARTY: Because Saffron fixed it.

BIANCA: Saffron fixed it?

MARTY: Yeah. After my bath. I asked her to fix it, and she did.

BIANCA: Saffron fixed it? Saffron the internet genius fixed it? Saffron's from India, Marty. She's a retard. She can't even give you a bath properly.

MARTY: No, she—

BIANCA: She always burns you with the hot water. She's totally retarded.

MARTY: No, she—she—

BIANCA: *What*, Marty? What?

MARTY: Nothing. Just—she's not retarded.

BIANCA: Oh? Oh, isn't she?

MARTY: And she doesn't burn me anymore.

BIANCA: Oh! Well!

MARTY: She's got the water really good / now.

BIANCA: That's great then! Saffron fixed the internet! Saffron gives you perfect baths! I guess Saffron's just perfect! She's the perfect woman!

MARTY: That's not—unnhh…

MARTY *grimaces—a shot of pain.*

BIANCA: Whatever, Marty. I don't give a shit.

MARTY: No, it wasn't—

BIANCA: I DON'T CARE, MARTY!

Eat your dinner.

Pause. MARTY *has his eyes closed, gritting his teeth.*

EAT YOUR DINNER, MARTY!

Pause.

What are you doing?

MARTY: My foot.

BIANCA: Your foot isn't sore.

MARTY: It is.

BIANCA: No it isn't.

MARTY: It is.

BIANCA: Your foot is gone.

MARTY: It still hurts.

BIANCA: No it doesn't, because it's not even there.

MARTY: Can I have an Endone?

Pause.

Please.

Please, Bianca.

BIANCA: Just for the record, Marty—Saffron doesn't actually like you. You know that, don't you? If she wasn't paid she wouldn't come. She wouldn't visit you. She finds you gross. Did you know that?

MARTY: Yes.

BIANCA: She finds you so gross. I've actually seen her gag. When she's washing out the crap, all the dried crap out from under your folds, from around your butt-hole. I've seen her gag. I've seen her try not to vomit. And I feel sorry for her. Because if she wasn't from India she wouldn't have to do this. She wouldn't have to give you baths, or wipe your butt. But this is what she has to do. All for money. All so she can feed her family.

Isn't that sad?

MARTY: Yes.

BIANCA: It's so sad. It makes me so sad for her. Does it make you sad for her, Marty?

MARTY: Yes.

BIANCA: Do you feel sorry for her?

MARTY: Yes. I do.

BIANCA: So do I.

Pause.

You haven't finished your pie.

MARTY: I'm not hungry.

BIANCA: I thought you wanted an Endone.

Pause.

BIANCA *gets some pie on the fork.*

Pause. Then, MARTY *opens his mouth.*

BIANCA *spoons the pie in.*

2. FLOUR

Spandau Ballet's 'True' starts to play.

PHILLIP *is illuminated in a spotlight wearing a dancer's leotard. He starts performing terrible ballet choreography. He is about 14 years old.*

MR LLEYLAND *appears, behind a counter. He has sweat patches under his arms.*

MR LLEYLAND: It's an all-boys school where I teach. And the last thing you can do, at an all-boys school, is like boys. At all—more than that—you've got to hate them. And that's the thing. I do. I do hate them.

So why do I… why do I have this… guilt, all the time?

Why do I have this guilt?

*The classroom. A cacophony.**

[*Louder*] Pay attention please. Quiet please. Talk time is over, okay? We're starting now, okay? Um—please—um—now—have you all got your ingredients?—Excuse me?—Have you got your ingredients?—Did everyone get a—? Um, okay—have you got your homework sheet? Um—have you all got your ingredients?… All got your containers?… Your homework?—Um—listen, please, um… Boys! Silence, please! Um—Ten… nine… eight… seven… six… —BOYS!

---

* In the original production the 'cacophony' was realised by hooking up a microphone to a guitar delay pedal. This looped Mr Lleyland's own words into a wall of sound, and the louder he spoke the louder it became.

PHILLIP: Mr Lleyland.

MR LLEYLAND: Yes? Phillip?

PHILLIP: I wasn't here on Tuesday.

MR LLEYLAND: Right. So you don't have the homework sheet?

PHILLIP: I have the homework sheet.

MR LLEYLAND: You… Right. Do you have your container?

PHILLIP: Yes.

MR LLEYLAND: Do you have your ingredients?

PHILLIP: Yes.

MR LLEYLAND: Do you have the homework sheet?

PHILLIP: I said yes.

MR LLEYLAND: Right—but you weren't here on Tuesday.

PHILLIP: Chris brought it over.

MR LLEYLAND: Did he?

PHILLIP: He comes over to my house sometimes.

MR LLEYLAND: Great. Well, if you / want to—

PHILLIP: To swim in the pool.

MR LLEYLAND: Okay.

PHILLIP: And wrestle.

Beat.

MR LLEYLAND: Okay. Um.
Well, I should / go and help…

PHILLIP: Yes, you should help the other students now. Here's my sheet.

MR LLEYLAND: Thank you.
Is that a phone number?

PHILLIP: In case you have any questions.

MR LLEYLAND: Pardon?

PHILLIP: About my answers.

MR LLEYLAND: I'm not sure I / follow—

PHILLIP: Like question 12.

MR LLEYLAND: 'The chilli plant was not always a flavouring. What was its original purpose?'
You wrote, 'I'm really, really hard right now'.

Pause.

Okay, um. Phillip—that's—that's not the correct answer.

GERALD *appears. He is a big, bearded gay bear, in a pink, frilly apron.*

GERALD: Because if there's one thing I just love—if there's one thing that really makes me happy—it's cooking for my husband. My hubby-cub. Because when I bake my cakes, my flambé, my crêpes… When I bake for him, I sprinkle everything with love. I sprinkle it with love, I sprinkle it with trust, I sprinkle it with sprinkles. And when we eat, it fills my heart with love. Plus it makes the house smell like cinnamon, and I do love cinnamon.

Home.

MR LLEYLAND *enters.*

Sweetie.

MR LLEYLAND: Hi, sweetie.

GERALD: Smells good, doesn't it?

MR LLEYLAND: Mmm, cinnamon.

GERALD: Mmm, cinnamon! Give me a hug!

GERALD *grabs him in a bear hug.*

Grrr!

MR LLEYLAND: Grrr.

GERALD: How was school, little boy?

MR LLEYLAND: It was okay.

GERALD: Were they nice to you?

MR LLEYLAND: I can't control them.

GERALD: Oh! Monsters!

MR LLEYLAND: I think it's the recipes.

GERALD: No! Those muffins are yummy!

MR LLEYLAND: I don't think 14-year-olds want muffins.

GERALD: Well, what do they want then?

MR LLEYLAND: They want to… I don't know. They want to finger every girl they see.

GERALD: [*giggling*] Stop it!

MR LLEYLAND: I can't keep doing it, it's pathetic.

GERALD: Sweetie.

MR LLEYLAND: I should quit.

GERALD: No! You just tell them they better be good, or you'll pull them over your knee and smack their little bottoms!

MR LLEYLAND: Oh my God.

GERALD: Crack a smile, sourpuss!

He tries to tickle MR LLEYLAND*'s belly.*

Go on—give us a grin, you old maid!

GERALD *disappears.*

MR LLEYLAND: [*whispered*] In control, in control.

A pot rattles.

[*Whispered*] Quiet.

There is a pause—a tension grows between the pot and MR LLEYLAND. *Then—the pot is slammed and he yells…*

Quiet!

The classroom. A cacophony.

Okay, um, excuse me—okay, excuse me, um, does everyone—does everyone have their containers?—Because… um, there's still sheets up here, so everyone—everyone needs a sheet—does anyone not have a container?—Does anyone not have a sheet?—If you've got your ingredients you can—um—

PHILLIP: Mr Lleyland.

Pause.

MR LLEYLAND: Yes?

PHILLIP: My oven isn't on.

MR LLEYLAND: It's not pre-heated?

PHILLIP: It's not on.

MR LLEYLAND: Someone turned it off?

PHILLIP: I'll use yours instead.

MR LLEYLAND: Yes, you can use mine. That should be alright.

PHILLIP *starts cutting a knob of butter.*

PHILLIP: That's better. We can talk now. Did you see me in the talent show?

MR LLEYLAND: Okay, um, yes—I went to the talent show.

PHILLIP: Did I look good?

MR LLEYLAND: I'm sorry?

PHILLIP: I was wearing a leotard.

MR LLEYLAND: Yes. I know. I—

PHILLIP: Did I look good? In my leotard?

MR LLEYLAND: I thought your, your dancing… I thought your dancing was good.

Pause.

PHILLIP *stares at* MR LLEYLAND, *unrelenting.*

I don't know much about dancing.

PHILLIP: You didn't like it?

MR LLEYLAND: No, I—I liked it, I just—

PHILLIP: I thought so.

MR LLEYLAND: No—but not like—

PHILLIP: You didn't like it?

MR LLEYLAND: No—I did! I just / didn't—

PHILLIP: I thought so.

MR LLEYLAND: Excuse me, I have to / help the—

PHILLIP: Help the other students? Go ahead.

He dumps a bag of flour into a bowl. It explodes in a white cloud and covers them both.

Oops.

MR LLEYLAND: [*loudly*] That's alright, Phillip! It's just a mistake!

PHILLIP: Pass me the condensed milk.

MR LLEYLAND *hands it to him.*

MR LLEYLAND: I should get a—a sponge or—I'll get a cloth or—

PHILLIP *opens the can and dips in a spoon.*

PHILLIP: I love condensed milk.

MR LLEYLAND: Don't fool around, Phillip.

PHILLIP: It's sweet and creamy.

MR LLEYLAND: That's for the recipe.

PHILLIP *holds the spoon up to* MR LLEYLAND.

PHILLIP: Want a try?

MR LLEYLAND: I—I—that is inappropriate.

PHILLIP: Maybe you'd prefer—

PHILLIP *dips in his finger and holds it up.*

MR LLEYLAND: I'd—I'd—I have to help the other—

PHILLIP *wipes the condensed milk across* MR LLEYLAND*'s bottom lip. Then, he disappears.*

GERALD *appears.*

GERALD: Honey?

Pause.

What's the matter?

Pause.

Want a hug?

MR LLEYLAND: I don't think even a hug can help me now.

GERALD: You're sweating buckets.

MR LLEYLAND: I always sweat.

GERALD: Not this much. Are you sick?

MR LLEYLAND: Yes. I'm sick. I'm very, very sick.

GERALD: I'm going to make you a big batch of hot chicken soup—that's what I'm going to do. That's food for the soul.

MR LLEYLAND: I tried, Gerald.

GERALD: Honey?

MR LLEYLAND: I tried so hard. I skipped yard duty. I didn't make eye contact. I never went to one swimming carnival. But it's no good. I'm an animal.

GERALD: Of course you're an animal! You're a bear! Grrr!

MR LLEYLAND: Please stop it. You don't know. You don't know how sick, how sick I—I—

GERALD: I don't care, sweetie. I love you.

MR LLEYLAND: But you could find someone else.

GERALD: Honey!

MR LLEYLAND: You could find someone younger.

GERALD: Honey! Look at me! I don't want some stupid little twinkie.

Twinkies aren't a meal. I want a big slab of a man—that's what I want. I want you.

MR LLEYLAND: But I'm so old. I'm so old and so sick / and so—

GERALD: You're not old. You're not sick. You're my fuzzy little husbear and we're good together, aren't we?

MR LLEYLAND: Yes.

GERALD: Tell me how good we are.

MR LLEYLAND: We're so good…

GERALD: That's what I told my parents, remember? When I was 40, I said to them—'Mum and Dad—I'm a bear. I am a hairy, older gay man. I like barbecues and bowling and snuggling up in tents and I'm proud.'

MR LLEYLAND: And your mother cried.

GERALD: And my father never looked at me again. But it doesn't matter. Because I've got you. And as long as I've got you I've got all I need in the world.

What's wrong, sweetie?

MR LLEYLAND: Everything.

GERALD: Well, you know what? I'm going to bake you a cake.

GERALD *disappears.*

PHILLIP *re-appears.*

The classroom. Quiet, at last. Spandau Ballet's 'True' starts to play again.

PHILLIP: Mr Lleyland.

MR LLEYLAND: Yes?

PHILLIP: I can't knead the dough.

MR LLEYLAND: Do you need help?

PHILLIP: I need you to show me.

MR LLEYLAND *starts kneading the dough.*

MR LLEYLAND: Just roll it gently.

PHILLIP *places his hands in it too.*

PHILLIP: Like this.

MR LLEYLAND: Just like that. Exactly.

3. SUGAR

PRISCILLA—*a 14-year-old girl in standard-issue private school uniform. Her hair is a black curly lump on her head, with a curly spool of fringe. She isn't terribly unattractive, but has bad posture and some pimples and is generally covered in loser dust. When she speaks her teeth are visible. They are horrible beyond belief, totally black and decaying.*

PRISCILLA: Wow yeah hey okay so top ten—top ten…

She gets suddenly woozy, then unwraps a candy bar and scarfs it so fast it's unbelievable.

[*Re-energised*] So yeah basically top ten candy bars in reverse order starting with least delicious and climaxing with most delicious of all ten on the count of five, ready, one-two-three-four-five, okay so—[*counting on her fingers*] Kit Kat, Mars, Dairy Milk Hazelnut, Dairy Milk Walnut, Time Out, Boost, Flake, Spearmint Aero, Milky Way with Smarties, and Peppermint Crisp number one, yeah, Peppermint Crisp my number one, so what?, but most people say that's weird and most people are like, 'Priscilla are you weird or what?' but no shut up 'cause when I was really little, see, my mum used to make this chocolate mousse where she'd grate up Peppermint Crisp with the cheese grater and ohmygod drool I'd lick the bowl and the mixing spoon and anything else it even touched like my sleeve or the floor like lick it dry like nothing you've ever ohmygod—lick-lick-lick, so good, mmm, so good, pant!—and that's why I'm totally retarded for Peppermint Crisp, that's why I'm on six bars a day although I gotta say, and I do gotta say this, it does hurt my teeth—it really hurts my teeth—its texture, the crunchiness well babe that's just glass, broken glass with the teeth I got, see, it's totally embarrassing and totally retarded but I never brushed them from the age of zero and I know I was supposed to and I know at some point someone showed me how or whatever, but no, no, and I didn't, not ever, and right now see I got a mouth fulla nubs and its weird I just gotta say it's so weird how small your teeth are, how big they are to me in my head and the mirror when I smile all black and gross but then this tiny bit of bone all yellow in my hand if I bite into an apple or a pear or something but babe you gotta know now that's not on the top of my food chain, apples and fruit and shit no way babe that stuff's spew, that stuff I eat in the car on the way to the dentist, last-ditch on the way to the dentist like 'hmm maybe this apple will save my whole entire life' with Mum in the front like 'blah-blah dentist's bills, blah-blah orthodontist bills, blah-blah school bills' like shut up, bitch, whatever, stick a fucking apple in your own mouth and shut the fuck up bitch 'cause yeah it costs to see the dentist and yeah that's money whoopee but I'm your daughter bitch and I'm sorry but doesn't it trouble you on any level, doesn't it disturb you on any level that my mouth is a fucking swamp 'cause YOU let me scarf all the candy I could eat from the moment I was a foetus practically, left me alone, left me scarfing so you could work at the old people's home peeling skin off grapes for old cunts and I'm sorry you couldn't get it together to smell my breath and I'm sorry you couldn't get it together to brush my teeth but seriously bitch it's not like you pay for this school, it's not like you pay for anything 'cause I did the study, I got the scholarship, I got the job in the school canteen recess and lunchtimes and clean-ups after school elbow-deep in fryer grease and nose-deep in cringe ohmygod humiliation bitch to pay for the dentures you won't buy me, BITCH!

Pause.

The canteen is okay actually.

Pause.

Like, the work sucks and sometimes the girls are bitches and sometimes they're all like 'Can I have a bag of lolly teeth, Princilla'…
But the boys, ohmygod, the boys.

Pause.

Okay so ready so like okay so top boys in my school in reverse order starting with least cutest and climaxing with most cutest of all ten on the count of five, ready, one-two-three-four-five, okay so—tenth place is Tom Meadow, he gets a pastie sometimes, Jamie Barlow number nine, three cans of Pepsi a day, eighth Alex Wu, total hottie on swim team in Speedos but his lunch gets packed, boo, number seven Jordan Hill, chicken rolls with beetroot, six is Cameron Prescott, chocolate cookie sometimes $2.60 but he's a dick, such a dick, a hot dick but a mean dick 'cause in Year Seven he taped a condom to my back in sex ed, Nick Olivio number five meat pie with sauce, total sweetie, total hottie, helped me when I slipped down a mudbank, Mark Bailey number four he gets Redskins 'cause they're 50 cents and he's scholarship like me, then there's Aaron Leskie who's not like me 'cause he's the richest kid on the planet even though he doesn't eat anything from the canteen, number two Mike Arnold and ohmygod, seriously, he seriously looks so much like Taylor Lautner it's not even funny but actually it is kinda funny 'cause Mike thinks Taylor Lautner is a fag, but now it's, like, drum roll number one and you already guessed it babe—you've got to guess it—shhh… ready?— [*whispering*] It's Troy—ohmygod—Troy McMahon—ohmygod—can you even hear his name over my drooling?!—Ohmygod, so hot, so raunch, so deep, so sad, like really deep and really sad 'cause he's got a sick dad and heaps of feelings, and one time I nearly even saw him cry even, like awwww, babe, lemme wipe those tears, lemme swoon times infinity Troy McMahon, boy of my dreams, number one crush with a bullet through my heart…

Sausage roll, no sauce.

TROY *appears.*

TROY: Sausage roll.

PRISCILLA: Hey, how's it going?

TROY: Yeah, good. No sauce.

PRISCILLA: How's your dad doing?

TROY: What?

PRISCILLA: Your dad. I heard your dad was sick.

TROY: Uh. Yeah.

PRISCILLA: What's wrong with him?

TROY: He's got cancer.

PRISCILLA: Bad cancer?

TROY: Yeah.

PRISCILLA: All cancer is bad cancer, I guess.

TROY: Two dollars, right?

PRISCILLA: Is he gonna die?

TROY: Yeah.

PRISCILLA: Yeah, 'cause you know it's kind of weird 'cause my dad didn't die of cancer but he had another incurable disease which was HIV, well actually it was pneumonia 'cause of HIV, 'cause he was a heroin user in his youth and middle age, but sometimes it was medicinal, 'cause like it was methadone and he was prescribed it anyway, but he died when I was three so whatever, so like what do I know, right? All's I'm saying is I'm here if you want to talk about it or cry or something. Here's your sausage roll.

TROY: Um, there's sauce on it.

PRISCILLA: Ohmygod, I'm such a retard! Hang on—yeah, 'cause my mum and me were—

Another boy—CAMERON—*appears.*

CAMERON: Hurry up, faggot.

PRISCILLA: Cameron Prescott, sixth cutest boy when he's in gym shorts and if he's not talking or doing anything. Otherwise—butthole to the extreme.

TROY: She put sauce on it.

CAMERON: She put sauce on it? What the fuck is wrong with you, Priscilla?

PRISCILLA: I said I'm sorry! Jeez Louise!—Two dollars.

TROY *hands over the money.*

Thanks. 'Bye, Troy.

TROY: 'Bye.

PRISCILLA: Say hi to your dad for me.

TROY: Yeah…

They move away from PRISCILLA.

CAMERON: Man… the breath on that bitch.

TROY: I know. It's like, toxic—like—

CAMERON: Imagine getting head from that…

TROY *giggles.*

Like—you put your dick near her and it shrivels up… it drops off…

TROY: And you cum and you blast out like half her teeth…

CAMERON: [*giggling*] And she'd / be like—

TROY: She'd be like—

CAMERON: 'The tooth fairy's coming tonight!'

TROY *busts a gut.*

TROY: She'd be glad. [*In a bogan accent*] 'I'm gunna get some money!'

CAMERON: What a fucking dyke.

TROY: Man, I don't even want to eat this. I don't want to eat anything that bitch has touched.

They giggle. PRISCILLA *looks on with a dreamy expression and her hands clasped over her head. She chews on a Peppermint Crisp bar.*

PRISCILLA: Troy McMahon. And see it's like totally dumb 'cause I know I'm being like a total retard about this, right, 'cause yeah okay right so yeah he's way too good for me and way too hot and dreamy and right now you're all like 'bitch he'll never be your husband' and 'bitch what kind of a crush is that?' but wait a minute see 'cause you don't know me in a year's time babe, you don't know me then and that's only $1000 away now, only $1000 and I'm ready, I'm so ready, I've been measured, I've been fitted, I got two teeth I can keep on the bottom, and the dentures slip, they slip in babe and I'm transformed forever and ever, phoenix from the ashes, ugly duckling to beautiful swan, art geek to prom queen and that tinsel crown is mine bitch and so's Troy McMahon when I'm gleaming white gum to gum, gleaming white in my mouth and his perfect face perfect reflected staring in my teeth all like— [*gazing into the Peppermint Crisp*] 'I love you, Priscilla, you and me and all your teeth together forever' and it's real, huh, practically, like when he kisses me it'll be just that sweet I know it, sweet peppermint kiss and his spit will be sweet as sugar I know, I know it and I'll suck his tongue like a gobstopper—ohmygod swoon together ohmygod forever, and one day, one day finally Troy will be like…

TROY: Sausage roll, no sauce.

PRISCILLA: … and I'll be like 'coolio schmoolio babe and how's your dad?'

TROY: He died.

Pause.

PRISCILLA: Jesus H. Christ.

TROY: Yeah.

PRISCILLA *gets a sausage roll and squirts sauce on it as she talks.*

PRISCILLA: Yeah 'cause it's like when my dad died I can't remember it but I was… I was sad. Like, sad for a three-year-old which means I probably just cried or something. Are you sad?

TROY: Yeah.

PRISCILLA: Have you been crying, Troy?

TROY: Shut the fuck up, Priscilla.

Pause.

PRISCILLA: Okay, sorry. Just asking, that's all. Just—like—I'm here if you want to talk to someone, / that's all.

TROY: Fuck off, Priscilla.

PRISCILLA: Okay, sorry. / Two dollars.

TROY: [*yelling*] WHAT THE FUCK, PRISCILLA?

PRISCILLA: What?!

TROY: I SAID NO SAUCE!

He throws the sausage roll at PRISCILLA *as hard as he can. Sauce and meat explode all over her.*

TROY *disappears.*

Dripping in meat and pastry, PRISCILLA *stares at the audience.*

TRUFFLES

An elaborate dinner is set for two: gleaming rows of cutlery, crystal glasses, a champagne bottle in silver bucket with ice.

Standing at either side of the table: DE SILVA *and* DOROTHY.

DE SILVA *is dressed like A Businessman*

DOROTHY *is dressed like A Whore.*

DOROTHY & DE SILVA: [*in unison*] A whore and a businessman walk into a restaurant.

There is a burst of canned laughter and they sit down.

Pause.

Then…

DE SILVA: So, a businessman goes up to this whore.

DOROTHY: Oh, Christ no.

DE SILVA: Goes up to this whore and says, 'What can I get for $10?'

DOROTHY: I don't want to hear this.

DE SILVA: Whore goes, 'I'll show you what you can get for $10', and she takes him up to the hotel room—they're at a hotel, by the way.

DOROTHY: Right.

DE SILVA: So, she takes him up to the hotel room and she fucks his brains out. Fucks his brains right out of his head. All sorts of crazy shit.

DOROTHY: Ten bucks worth, uh-huh.

DE SILVA: And he's happy. And he's a-singing. But then the next day…
He starts itching.
His balls are on fire.
He's caught, he's caught…

DOROTHY: He's itching. / I got you.

DE SILVA: Crabs. He's got crabs. So he goes back to this whore—*furious*! He goes back to this whore and he screams at her, he goes, 'You fucking whore! You gave me crabs! You gave me fucking crabs.'
And the whore looks at him.
She looks him up and down. And then she goes, 'Crabs, huh? Well, what did you expect for 10 bucks? Lobster?'

Pause.

DOROTHY: That joke isn't funny.

DE SILVA: Yes it is.

DE SILVA *hits a dinner bell.*

†

Silence.

After a few moments, DOROTHY *lights a cigarette. She barely gets one drag before* DE SILVA *reaches across the table, plucks it from her mouth, then drops it into her wine glass.*

Then, DE SILVA *hits the bell.*

†

DE SILVA: You're going to enjoy this dinner, Dorothy.

DOROTHY: Am I?

DE SILVA: You're really going to enjoy this dinner.

DOROTHY: That so?

DE SILVA: The chef, this guy Mitoro… he's got three Michelin-star restaurants in London. Two in Singapore. How do you like that?

DOROTHY: I like that fine.

DE SILVA: So…
You know.
This. This is… This is something, Dorothy.
Not anyone could do this.

DOROTHY: Do what?

DE SILVA: This. *This*. Not everyone could buy out this place out for the night. Not anyone could pull this off.

DOROTHY: I understand.

DE SILVA: Do you?

DOROTHY: You're a very important man.

DE SILVA: You're really going to enjoy this dinner.

DOROTHY: Am I?

DE SILVA: Yes. You are.

DOROTHY: Well.
We'll see.

DE SILVA *hits the bell.*

†

Silence.

Then, DE SILVA *hits the bell.*

†

DOROTHY: Because I'm a hooker. Because I don't like hooker jokes. Because I don't like… Jokes. At all. Actually.

DE SILVA: You don't like jokes?

DOROTHY: No.

DE SILVA: You don't like *jokes*?

DOROTHY: NO!

DE SILVA: Well, what would you say, Dorothy… What exactly would you say is your taste in humour, then?

DOROTHY *shrugs.*

Well, I'm sorry, but you'll have to be a little more talkative. That's the deal. I don't want silence. I want this to be a nice, civil dinner between adults. And if you're going to sit there—your legs crossed, your cigarette in your mouth… If you're not going to fill the silence—then I'll do it. And I'll fill it with whatever I want. You understand?

Pause.

A whore and a mule—

DOROTHY: How was your day?

DE SILVA *hits the bell.*

†

DE SILVA: —and that's only half of it. I mean, that's only half of the shit he does to… to… undermine me. Every day. I mean, it. Every day. I have to… Right in front of my…
My…

He trails off as DOROTHY *does an enormous yawn.*

It goes for ages.

Then…

DOROTHY: Sorry? You were saying?

DE SILVA: Oh, nothing. Nothing. Nothing at all. And what about your day, Dorothy? How was your day?

DOROTHY: Okay.

DE SILVA: 'Okay?'

DOROTHY: You don't want to hear about my day.

DE SILVA: Oh, but of course I do. It must have been so much more exciting than mine. Do tell. Please.

Beat.

DOROTHY: Alright.

So, my day was going fine, yeah? Good day. Whatever-day. And then this prick comes in. This truck-driving prick.

DE SILVA: I see. And what did this truck-driving prick do?

DOROTHY: Well, he asked me if he could fuck me in the ass, and I said, 'Sure, you can fuck me in the ass'—but then he didn't take the condom off when he stuck it in my pussy.

So I got all shit in there. You know?

DE SILVA: Right.

DOROTHY: Got all shit in my / pussy.

DE SILVA: Right.

DOROTHY: Right up there. Right up in my pussy. Shit. In my pussy, you know?

DE SILVA: *Dorothy.*

DOROTHY: And so I started yelling, and Marcus heard me and he just went ape shit. Came in and hit the guy with a claw hammer, this hammer he keeps for hitting guys, / you know?

DE SILVA: DOROTHY.

DOROTHY: So we got an extra hundred out of the prick but it still itches like a / fucking—

DE SILVA *hits the bell.*

†

DOROTHY *is giggling.*

DE SILVA: You liked that one?

DOROTHY: It wasn't bad.

DE SILVA: Well. Just goes to show. When you try new things, Dorothy…

DOROTHY: Don't push it.

DE SILVA: Shall we order?

DOROTHY: Oh. Sure. Just give me a sec… I haven't even—

DE SILVA: Let us peruse the menu. For your benefit.

He picks up the menu and reads.

Now…

Entrée.

That's French for 'appetisers'…

DOROTHY: 'Entrée'—in its direct translation—is 'entry'.

Pause. DE SILVA *stares at her.*

DE SILVA: Warm oysters with julie… [*mispronouncing*] julienned—

DOROTHY: [*pronouncing correctly*] Julienned.

DE SILVA: Julienned vegetables, pernod and caviar…
Quail with rose petals and cactus pears…
[*Mispronouncing*] Shirred egg—

DOROTHY: [*correctly*] Shirred.

DE SILVA: White truffles and baby potatoes.
Mains: Goat cheese and artichoke ravioli, with a red beet [*mispronouncing*] di-jon jus—

DOROTHY: [*correctly*] Dijon. Jus.

DE SILVA: Shut up… Lobster [*mispronouncing*] vahiné—

DOROTHY: [*correctly*] Vahiné—

DE SILVA: Wait, no— [*mispronouncing*] Aragosta—alla—

DOROTHY: [*correctly*] Aragosta—

DE SILVA: [*mispronouncing*] —alla vahiné… / Aragosta—

DOROTHY: [*correctly*] Aragosta alla vahiné.

DE SILVA *slams his hand down on the bell.*

†

There is a small amber-coloured bottle on the table, with a bright label. A thick, syrupy liquid.

DOROTHY: Robitussin.

DE SILVA: Robitussin, like—?

DOROTHY: Cough syrup.

DE SILVA: Right.

DOROTHY *pours two glasses from it.*

DOROTHY: Bottoms up.

She goes 'cheers' with the glass. DE SILVA *doesn't.*

What? Are you scared?

DE SILVA: It's cough syrup.

DOROTHY: Yeah. I said that already.
DE SILVA: Why would we drink cough syrup?
DOROTHY: Grow a dick, okay?

She drinks her glass down in one huge gulp.

Then, DE SILVA *does the same—retching.*

He hits the bell.

†

Pause.

DE SILVA: What would you consider to be an aphrodisiac?
DOROTHY: Stuff that makes you horny?
DE SILVA: Food, actually. Not 'stuff'. Food.
So money doesn't count.
DOROTHY: FUCK / YOU!

DE SILVA *hits the bell.*

†

DE SILVA: Give it to me.
DOROTHY: No.
DE SILVA: Give it to me.
DOROTHY: No.
DE SILVA: Give me that watch, Dorothy. It's impolite.
DOROTHY: I said I won't look again.
DE SILVA: Yes, you did say that. But you also said that 20 minutes ago.
So give it to me. Now.

Pause.

Do you want me to make a call?

Pause.

DOROTHY *takes off her watch and hands it to him.*

You can have it back when I'm done with you.
DOROTHY: When you're done with me.
DE SILVA: Exactly.
DOROTHY: When you're done with me.

DE SILVA: Right.

DE SILVA *hits the bell.*

†

Pause.

DE SILVA *starts rubbing his eyes and giggling a little.*

This sets DOROTHY *off. She starts giggling.*

He giggles at her giggling. She giggles at him giggling at her giggling.

They explode into laughter, wiping away tears, stoned out of their minds.

Then…

DE SILVA: I, I, I… You know, I find you incredibly unattractive.

Beat.

DE SILVA *hits the bell.*

†

They are both laughing hysterically.

DOROTHY: … And I don't even know why he thought… Why he thought I'd like it, but— / but—

DE SILVA: You know there's this mushroom…

DOROTHY: Oh, yeah?

DE SILVA: I read, on the—Wikipedia or something—I read about this special kind of mushroom… If a woman smells it—if she smells this mushroom, she'll just… cum. Just like that. Like POW!—orgasm. But a man… if a man smells it… this same mushroom… it just, stinks… like the worst shit in the world.
What do you think of that, Dorothy?

DOROTHY: What do I think?

DE SILVA: Yes. What do you think… philosophically… about that mushroom?

DOROTHY: I think… men… women… whatever. Truth is, if a woman stuck that mushroom up her pussy, you'd still wanna sniff it. I can guarantee it. You and every other man in this fucking world / would—

DE SILVA: I don't think / that's—

DOROTHY: I can guarantee it. I can GUARANTEE it. If I stuck that mushroom up my pussy right now, you would kneel there sniffing it for the rest of your shitty life, / I can—

DE SILVA *hits the bell.*

†

DOROTHY *is bored.*

DE SILVA: I'm just saying there's… there's pressure. You know. Pressure. Everywhere.

DOROTHY: Yuh-huh.

DE SILVA: When you have a high-pressure job. When there are… older people, above you. Waiting for you to fail. When there are younger people below you. Waiting for you to fail.

DOROTHY: Yuh-huh.

DE SILVA: When there are… expectations of you. As an employee. As a husband. You see how hard it can be, how hard, as a man, to live, and to—to…

DOROTHY *yells over her shoulder...*

DOROTHY: CAN WE ORDER PLEASE?!

... then hits the bell.

†

DE SILVA *is masturbating, desperately trying to get a hard-on.*

DOROTHY *sits, smoking, turned away, trying to avoid looking.*

After a while…

DOROTHY: Do you want me to—?

DE SILVA: DON'T. TALK!

DOROTHY *resumes her smoking.*

DE SILVA *continues masturbating, for a while.*

Then, he gives up and taps the bell.

†

DE SILVA *sits in the same position, now with his pants buttoned up.*

DOROTHY *sips from her cough syrup.*

A long pause.

Then…

DOROTHY: Well. At least food was good.
DE SILVA: YOU FUCKING—

DE SILVA *slams his fist on the table, as* DOROTHY *taps the bell.*

†

DE SILVA: [*screaming*] BITCH!

DE SILVA *rings the bell.*

†

DE SILVA: BITCH!

He rings the bell.

†

DE SILVA: BITCH!

He rings the bell.

†

DE SILVA: BITCH!

He rings the bell.

†

DE SILVA: BITCH!

He rings the bell.

†

DE SILVA: BITCH!

DOROTHY *throws her drink in his face.*

Then, she rings the bell.

†

Three empty bottles of cough syrup on the table.

DOROTHY *lights another cigarette.*

DOROTHY: It's not my real name.

DE SILVA: Well, you know… I did guess that.

DOROTHY: Everyone in the family, Mum and Dad, my brothers and sisters—they all called me Dorothy, because I loved *The Wizard of Oz*. It was all I'd watch. With Dad—sitting with my dad, in a big armchair. Drinking Milo, eating toast, watching *Wizard of Oz*. He'd play with my hair. Call me 'Dorothy'—in the witch's voice. Like, 'DO-ROTHY. DO-ROTHY.' Fuck those were good days. When we were kids, hey. What the fuck happens to us? What happens between then and now?

Pause.

DE SILVA: You know the lion was a faggot. In that movie.

DOROTHY: Yeah.

DE SILVA: One of those things you don't realise. Till you're older. But then you look back.

Pause.

[*Grinning*] What a faggot that lion was.

DE SILVA *rings the bell.*

†

They are screaming at one another.

DE SILVA: SHUT UP, DOROTHY! SHUT UP! SHUT UP! JUST SHUT THE FUCK UP!

DOROTHY: [*loudly*] For fuck's sake!

DE SILVA: SHUT THE FUCK UP!

DOROTHY: You think it was a big deal?!

DE SILVA: JUST SHUT THE FUCK UP!

DOROTHY: You think it was a big deal?!

DE SILVA: Why won't she shut the fuck up?

DOROTHY: I have a guy who pays me to / spit in his mouth.

DE SILVA: Shut the fuck up.

DOROTHY: I have a guy, / a guy just like you—

DE SILVA: Shut the fuck up.

DOROTHY: —who pays me to kick him in / the balls.

DE SILVA: Shut the fuck up.

DOROTHY: / In the fucking BALLS! AND YOU STILL THINK—

DE SILVA: SHUT THE FUCK UP!

DOROTHY: / YOU HONESTLY THINK—

DE SILVA: SHUTTHEFUCKUPSHUTTHEFUCKUPSHUTTHEFUCK—

DOROTHY: —YOUR SOFT DICK IS SOME BIG PROBLEM FOR ME?!

DE SILVA *slams his fist on the table and stands up.*

DOROTHY *rings the bell—the scene does not change.*

She rings it again, frantically.

He advances on her.

She rings it again.

He sweeps the cutlery off the table—the bell goes with it.

DE SILVA *grabs* DOROTHY *by back of the hair and slams her headfirst into the table.*

She bounces back off the table and into her chair, looking up at him, stunned.

He stares back at her.

Then, he sits back down, and tucks a napkin into his shirt like a bib.

DE SILVA: You're really going to enjoy this meal.

THE END